Bringing the World t<

Bringing the World to your Church

A rescue pack of ideas and information
for missions mobilisers

Joy Piper

Acknowledgements

I owe a great deal to the many individuals and organisations who gave me ideas, information and prayerful support as I researched and wrote this book. I could not have completed it without their generosity, help and encouragement.
My thanks go especially to Stephen Passmore, whose request that I write him some guidelines for a world mission promoter inspired this book, and to my husband Brian and daughters Emma and Karen, who willingly tolerated considerable disruption to our family life whilst I wrote it.

Joy Piper has asserted her right under the Copyright, Designs and Patents Act 1998 to be identified as Author of this Work.

Published by WEC Publications, Bulstrode, Gerrards Cross, Bucks SL9 8SZ England.

First edition 2001

ISBN 0 900828 82 X

Illustrations by Taffy Davies

Typeset and layout by Bernard White, Dartford, Kent

Contents

1

On your marks . . . get set . . .

Starting off:
initial evaluation and preparation

Some are asked. Others volunteer. A fortunate few will actually be given some form of job description. Most, however, will simply be left to get on with it. Although one of the lowest profile jobs in the average church, those who take on the job of mission co-ordinator do so with great personal commitment to the cause. Undaunted by the general apathy often encountered, they offer faithful service, sometimes for thirty years or more. When they feel it is time to hand on to somebody else, however, they are usually unable to do so since no-one is likely to volunteer to replace them. Not immediately anyway. It is not a popular job.

Its popularity may not be great, but its importance is. Mission co-ordinators are a key link between the church at home, missionary societies, the missionary and the church overseas. The job title may vary, but its importance does not.

Speaking from experience

'Important' is the last word I would have used to describe how I felt as a new missionary secretary. I was not given any working brief or guidance, and although I had been a Christian for about thirteen years at the time and was experienced in other areas of Christian service, I felt confused, inadequate and overwhelmed. All I was given was a cardboard box crammed with correspondence and memorabilia from previous mission events. My feelings of inadequacy were intensified when I met with more experienced supporters of world-mission at area meetings, since I found myself unable to understand the mission-speak which they used so confidently. It was as if I had suddenly become a member of a Christian sub-culture but with no initiation ceremony and no clear idea as to what was expected of me.

It has become obvious from what other people have shared that my experience of being left to muddle on alone is not unique.

It is my memories of those initial feelings of discomfort and my longing for a basic reference tool to help me that became the catalyst for this book. It has been written to encourage those who may be running out of ideas after years in the job and also those who are newly appointed and uncertain how to proceed. It is a pick'n'mix of information, suggestions and examples drawn from a variety of sources. You can select and adapt them to fit your own particular Christian environment.

I hope it will especially encourage those in isolated situations who find it difficult to travel to area meetings or meet with other mission mobilisers.

What makes an effective mission mobiliser?

The bad news is there are no magic formulae, instant fool-proof methods or short cuts to guarantee success. However, there are qualities like persistence, patience and imagination which will go a long way to making the job easier.

A genuine interest in overseas mission and the world at large and an abiding love for God and other people will provide powerful motivation to keep you going when the going gets tough.

Most important of all is faithfulness in prayer, constantly acknowledging your dependence upon God.

Defining terminology

Most of us know to our cost that words are powerful tools with great potential for being misunderstood and interpreted according to the listener's experiences and prejudices. Negative connotations attached to traditional titles have led to churches updating the words used to describe their workers, hence the plethora of trendy labels which have sprung up to describe those engaged in raising mission awareness: motivators, co-ordinators, chairmen and secretaries preside nowadays over 'mission action-groups', 'mission education teams', 'working groups', 'world-mission councils' and 'mission partnership groups'. These have replaced the familiar missionary secretary and missionary committee in many places.

What about you? Have you ever stopped to consider whether your title is associated with any negative imagery which might hamper your efforts? Are you satisfied that it clearly and adequately describes your role within the life of the church? If not, can you think of one which will be more readily understood in your social and cultural environment?

Job titles within the world of commerce and management are an important part of our present-day culture. It is helpful to keep up to date with appropriate terms which are in fashion and integrate them into our Christian context, if we are to make sense to young people and converts from an unchurched background.

Defining the job

Encouraging any Christian group to become actively involved with world-mission is significantly important but notoriously difficult. As if that were not enough to contend with, the task of a mission mobiliser is rarely defined since the job is assumed to be self-explanatory.

It is useful to put together a simple working brief, however, if you are to do a really effective job. Consultation with your predecessor and mission mobilisers in other local churches, as well as area representatives or headquarters staff of organisations with which you are linked will be helpful. Their ideas can be used together with input from the church leadership to form a basic job description.

The following example of a written point of reference[1] shows what areas may usefully be clarified in order to avoid ambiguities which could lead to conflict or misunderstanding.

Recognising the role of the leadership

The main impetus for world-mission support comes from the top. Here the battle for mission is won or lost.

Job title: MISSIONARY SECRETARY

Main purpose of the job:
- To co-ordinate and encourage the church's support for missionary activity through prayer, sharing information and practical support.

Key tasks:
- To make recommendations to the leadership concerning the church's giving to missionaries and missionary organisations, including the preparation of an annual budget for financial support of missionaries, where appropriate. (This should be done in consultation with the church treasurer if possible).
- To meet with those carrying out similar roles within other churches in the circuit.
- To organise activities which enable members to find out more about world-mission.
- To communicate prayer needs to leadership for inclusion in prayers at Sunday worship and smaller mid-week gatherings.
- To ensure regular communication with supported missionaries.
- To maintain missionary notice board and keep it up to date.
- To write short updates of missionary news for church newsheets or magazines.
- To report regularly to the leadership.

Responsibilities:
- To continue to keep the support of Christian workers as an important focus within the church's programme and awareness, and to ensure that any prayer needs are circulated.

The extent of the leadership's visible commitment to world-mission will be reflected in the level of enthusiasm shown by the rest of the group. Of course the personality and input of the mission mobiliser are also important, but without discernible back-up from the leaders you may find yourself fighting for a lost cause. So it is important to work with your leaders right from the start, consulting and co-operating with them as much as possible. This may be easier said than done.

It helps enormously if leaders have had positive first-hand experience of the mission-field or missionaries. Some may have visited missionaries linked with their church. Others may have acquired a global outlook from belonging to a missionary family or from close friends who have been missionaries. Some leaders may even have wanted to become missionaries themselves but health problems or other difficulties prevented them. If you are blessed with such as these you have a head start.

On the other hand, if your leaders do not appear to be particularly interested in world-mission, there may be significant reasons for their indifference. Maybe they have had an unhappy experience of life overseas or of people from other cultures. More probably it may simply be that the pressure of their present responsibilities makes them feel unable to take anything else on board.

All you can do in these cases is to be sensitive to where they are coming from, keep the channels of communication open between you, and prayerfully continue to look for ways to bring world-mission into both church and leaders' thinking.

Get help

Mobilising the church for world-mission is not a job for one person. Find out who else is mission-minded and ask them to pray with and for you. Then begin to form a team to work alongside you, if one does not already exist.

Some basic questions need to be sorted out when forming a new world-mission team:

- What areas of church life and what missionary organisations should be represented on the team?

- By what proceedure are members to be appointed and for how long a term of service?

- What will the different team members' areas of responsibility be?

- How often will the team meet?

- Who will chair their meetings?

- Will meetings be formally minuted?

- How far in advance should events and meetings be planned?

As with your personal working brief, it helps to have a written point of reference so everyone knows where they are.

Defining a policy – mission statements

The defining of a common purpose and vision can be a most enlightening and stimulating exercise for all the members of a world-mission team.

Such a statement may be expressed in a single sentence or may take the form of a detailed and comprehensive church policy. The text in the box below is part of a four-page mission statement and is a good expression of mission commitment and motivation.[2]

OUR MISSION TO THE WORLD

Responsibility lies with the Mission Link Executive and Forum:

1. To send out short and long term workers on a regular basis.

2. To support our missionaries, before, during and after their service.

3. To give generously to key mission agencies.

4. To continue to develop links with other churches around the world for mutual support and encouragement in our common task.

Conclusion:

It is our desire as a church to unite in God's mission to the world. Wherever you bear your witness for Jesus Christ in his world, we desire as a fellowship to be fully behind you.

If that work should involve you in paid Christian service, we would be glad to give opportunity for guidance and support as you fulfil your task.

Preparing an ongoing mission education and support programme

Commitment to mission is brought about through the working of the Holy Spirit in the lives and understanding of individuals. We can be part of that process by making the issues known, but ultimately the work is God's, not ours. All the bright ideas in the world will not change attitudes and develop consistent commitment and support as God can by his Spirit.

There is, however, obviously a place for putting time and effort into creating a well organised and thoughtful programme which can permeate your group's life at every level and inspire meaningful support for those who serve in specific ways overseas. God uses people to carry out his purposes and this is where you and your team are vital.

Once you get started, the possibilities are almost limitless.

Clearing out

Many mission mobilisers inherit an assortment of literature, resources and memorabilia. Deciding how much of this should be kept and what should be thrown out is best done straight away, or there will be an even bigger mound of paper to tackle later. Clearing out is a valuable way of discovering what has already been done with regard to raising the profile of world-mission. This will help you assess the group's understanding of what is involved in mission support and its level of interest.

Although having some record of what has been done over recent years is useful, you do not have to keep every leaflet, letter and magazine article. Many will be out of date and can be binned.

Initial preparation

Whether your church is only minimally involved in world-mission or renowned for its zeal, taking time out every so often as a team to think, pray and assess will be time well spent. It will help to ensure that what you plan will be effective and relevant to your present church environment.

Here are some points it might be helpful to consider.

1. *Global-think does not come naturally.* 'To be a Christian is to be a missionary.' This is the message emblazoned on a Catholic missions collecting-box. It says it all. Yet world-mission is generally seen as an optional extra for a few enthusiasts. It cannot be assumed to come naturally to most Christians, however well versed in Scriptures such as Matthew 28:19 they may appear to be. Sometimes the implications just do not seem to sink in or bear any visible fruit in their lives.

Sadly, despite the best efforts of missionary organisations and mission mobilisers over recent years, the average person in the pew still associates the word 'missionary' with some drably clothed, other-worldly anachronism of a figure, to be regarded with a certain amount of suspicion, kept at a safe distance or forgotten altogether. If they are ever prayed for, it is in vague uninformed terms: 'God bless all the missionaries in far-off lands.'

This situation can be frustrating when you are all fired-up and raring to go, but it is a fact which needs to be faced as you plan your strategy.

2. *Over-enthusiasm can be a turn-off.* The wise mission mobiliser will temper zeal with gentleness and patience, recognising that over-the-top efforts to raise the profile of world-mission cause people to back-off in embarrassment or for fear of being pressured.

'Softly, softly, catchee monkey.' Taking time first of all to build relationships and to listen to people helps win their trust and attention, both of which are essential if the message is to succeed in getting across.

Once you have gained their trust and attention it is important to remember that most people switch off when bombarded with a stream of information.

Focusing regularly on particular issues, personnel or projects is much more effective than trying to cover too many things at once. It may seem like scratching the surface, but little and often is more manageable for most people.

Where to begin

A huge range of possibilities awaits you and your church. At the time of writing there are approximately 5,340 missionaries from the UK serving in 180 countries with 269 UK-based missionary agencies, (this figure includes 108 Roman Catholic societies and orders).

A vast amount of information is available, along with many excellent resources to enable churches to be informed about and support those who are engaged in world-mission. It can be very confusing, especially if you are starting from scratch or want to broaden the extent of your support. How do you begin to select from among so many deserving causes?

It might be helpful to make a simple assessment of the church's thinking. Evaluating their level of global awareness and understanding of their role in world-mission helps you to see where things are going well, where there is room for improvement, and then to make appropriate plans.

Looking at the church's recent track-record is the most obvious place to start.

Circulating a basic questionnaire amongst the members can help you find out how many people already receive prayer letters from missionaries and organisations and their particular areas of interest. You could also use the questionnaire to invite suggestions for future projects to stimulate interest and ways to communicate information effectively.

Assessing your church

Which of the following pictures best describes your present position?

Picture 1. Your loyalty is primarily to your denominational society, and to other non-denominational societies.

- Your link missionaries are adopted from outside your church family.
- Mission education relies on visiting speakers supplied by a society.
- Involvement tends to be rather superficial and thinly spread.
- Your church members prefer to be onlookers, guided by mission agencies rather than 'owning' mission themselves.

Picture 2. Your church is centred on individuals rather than society-orientated.

- You are continually looking to send out missionaries from among your number.
- Your mission support is focused on members now based overseas, fostering a close relationship with them as a continuing part of your church family.
- You see yourselves as active partners with any mission agencies involved.
- Your aim is to be as directly involved as possible with world-mission.

Picture 3. You see world-mission as a question of partnership and inter-dependency.

- You see yourselves as an active part of the global family of Christ.
- Your aim is to work together with non-western churches wherever possible, and to your mutual benefit.
- Your understanding of world-mission goes beyond merely being a question of sending missionaries 'over there.'

Having established your present position, think about whether you see your commitment as being centred on:

- a country or continent
- on individuals whom you know
- on a specific type of missionary activity
- on a particular society

If a society is your preference:

- Do you want to give priority to a denominationally based society or would you prefer to support one of the specialised non-denominational societies?
- To what extent will your choice be influenced by the theological stance of a society?
- Do you want to limit your interest to societies with whom you are already connected through members serving with them or other natural points of contact?

Keeping up the impetus

Having set up your team, assessed your church's situation and made your choices as to who and what to commit yourself to in support, you now face the task of maintaining a consistent level of interest and support. This is the real challenge of your job.

Even in the keenest churches missionary interest tends to fluctuate. This was the case in one suburban church which, although having an excellent record of mission support, discovered that other issues were beginning to push overseas mission lower down on the church's agenda. Early action to define and remedy the situation, accompanied by prayer that God would deepen missionary interest throughout the church, resulted in changes and additions being made to the church's traditional mission programme. Subsequently there was an increase in the number of missionaries sent out from that congregation, and a consistent 15-20% growth in giving to mission work.

The work of a mission mobiliser is never done, but the endless scope, adventure and opportunities it offers guarantees it need never be boring.

Enough of the preliminaries. Let's go for it!

Further reading:

Ian E. Benson (ed.), *The Effective Sending Church,* booklet 7. The Missionary Training Series. (The Missionary Training Service, 1997).

Willis E. Garret *You Can Have a Successful Missionary Program in your Church,* (SIM, 1991).

Think Global, Act Local (Global Connections). A set of periodically updated information sheets on how to involve your church with the wider world.

Footnotes:

1 Quoted by permission of Cupid Green Methodist Church Council.

2 Quoted by permission of Bromley Baptist Church

'Go!'

Creating a basic framework of education and information-sharing

It was the monthly mission-focus midweek meeting; a meeting I dreaded as, being the missionary secretary, I was expected to lead it. This month I had spent several hours compiling a series of questions for a very basic general knowledge-style quiz about world-mission. I felt distinctly sick. There we sat in a small side room: the pastor (who seemed to know everything there was to know on the subject already), my husband (present solely out of loyalty to me and not particularly interested), and one other member. The clock ticked on past eight o'clock, and it was obvious that nobody else was going to join us. I took a deep breath, broke the silence, and the meeting began. I felt discouraged and frustrated. It all seemed to have been a total waste of time and effort.

I wonder if this strikes a chord in you.

Missionary meetings are not popular events

There is something about the addition of the word 'missionary' to a church event which keeps most people away. Perhaps the unpopularity of missionary meetings is indicative of the insular attitude which some say characterises our island race. Maybe the lack of interest is due to prejudice about the term 'missionary' or to negative experiences of past missionary events.

Another possible reason is the common failure to preach and teach mission on a regular basis in our churches.

The individual church's geographical and social context may also be a factor. One rural church made the point that 'when the next village was considered by locals to be in another world, inspiring concern for foreign continents was far from easy.'[1]

Finally, are we mission mobilisers partly to blame? Do we actually make time for prayer that God will inspire missionary interest and action in the lives of his children?

Mission education is not just special meetings

A comprehensive programme of mission education and support has two main facets.

Firstly, there is the encouragement of existing supporters. This primarily involves keeping up the information flow to fuel their interest, giving and praying.

Secondly, there is the recruitment of more supporters. This is hard work! Claiming the attention of that apathetic majority requires imagination, energy and persistence. It means presenting information in such a way that they are inspired to get involved in active support, prayer and giving. This cannot be achieved solely through holding the occasional traditional missionary meeting which, though valued by the committed few, rarely attracts the apathetic majority. To succeed with this group, missionary news and praying has to be made part of the content of the regular meetings held in the church, targeting people where they are, without any give-away title which might alert them and keep them away.

Beginning with Sundays

Sunday services provide a captive audience of both present and potential supporters. One of the most effective ways to incorporate overseas mission into everyone's thinking and praying is through regular information slots in the Sunday services. These slots must be brief and imaginatively presented if they are to turn people on rather than off. Five minutes is the maximum time for which to aim. It takes discipline and careful preparation to keep to this!

Visual aids

These are very important. We retain facts better when they are presented visually. Well-prepared acetates are an easy and effective way of giving information. They can be used to highlight a few main points from the latest prayer-letter (in large lower-case letters so children can read them too). Cartoons, mission job-opportunities and personnel needs, posters and even photographs, can be printed onto acetates at some cost. If printing is too expensive, line-drawings can be traced onto an acetate by hand. Photocopies can also be made using special acetates.

Acting it out

'Hear ye! Hear ye!' You or a volunteer could act as a town-crier (perhaps borrowing a hand-bell) and shout the latest news from a 'scroll'.

'Read all about it ...!' Set up a news-stand on the platform and shout out the latest headlines from your missionary. Don't forget to have copies of their letter on your stand for people to collect.

'Urgent news flash ...' Type out some news extracts from the latest letter you have received. As you begin your news-spot, get someone to rush in waving the typed sheet, shouting 'Fax!' or 'E-mail!'

Present short drama sketches with a global theme.

Active participation

Hold brief interviews with people who have overseas experience.
Divide people into teams for a short game or quiz.
Arrange a live telephone link with your missionaries, time difference permitting.

Prayers and songs

Teach the congregation a worship song from a church in another country. Or use one of the many topical prayers from around the world. (see p. 54 for details of books of liturgies and worship from other cultures.)

Book reviews

Ask someone to review a missionary biography or topical book which they have enjoyed. This goes down well near Christmas when people are looking for presents for Christian friends and relations.

Getting world-mission into the news-sheet

Regular service information slots can be supplemented with concise, readable contributions to church news-sheets or magazines featuring material relevant to that month's topic.

Making mission part of the prayer-time

Including world-mission concerns in the prayer-times during Sunday worship is also very important. At the church I attended as a student I soon learned the names and situations of their ten missionaries simply because they were all prayed for in every service.

Our aim as mission mobilisers is to encourage whoever leads the congregation in prayer to be aware of overseas issues. How about giving them a simple typed sheet with just one or two prayer points, first making sure it is does not contain unpronounceable names?

Midweek activities

The introduction of mission education into every level of church life will become a reality only if it is enthusiastically introduced into all the different organisations within the church.

Fred Stainthorpe writes: 'Each church has its own mid-week activities ... Small groups often engender enthusiasm and commitment to a cause and a person. So our ladies' meeting, house groups, young people's (and old people's) fellowships can play an important part by developing personal links with those serving abroad. Sanctified imagination can even find ways of introducing some missionary subject into our fringe groups.'[2]

Write down a list of all your church's organisations, how often they meet, who they are for, the leader's names and what format the meetings take. Getting to know the different leaders, asking them about their groups, showing an interest in what they are doing, and demonstrating a willingness to listen, all help to establish a good working relationship with them. Invite them to join the mission action-group's deliberations on a regular basis. This will help you to brainstorm world-mission education together, as a team.

Some groups will be only too glad to receive information about resources and potential speakers, whilst others may feel threatened by any suggestions offered to them by 'outsiders'. Not everyone may accept your initial invitation to join the mission-education team, but they may be won over later by other means, such as being asked to provide hospitality for visiting mission personnel. Another way to woo support from leaders is for the mission action-group to host an event especially for them. A buffet meal could be provided, followed by a fun mission-education exercise to do together. A table covered with samples of mission-education materials and backed by a display board could be put in one corner.

How about debating the importance, or not, of being involved with world-mission? You could set up a 'press conference' featuring guest experts from one of the organisations if you do not feel qualified to answer on-the-spot questions yourself. This would give people who are actually hostile towards the concept of world-mission the chance to air their views, and have them answered.

Ideas for specific groups

Once you have the co-operation and support of those who lead activities, you can proceed with filtering world-mission into all the different levels of church life.

Here are some ideas of how to introduce global issues into individual groups. They can be mixed and matched according to what works for you.

The ladies' meeting

Invite a speaker from a missionary or overseas agency, or someone who has visited overseas workers, helped out short-term, or worked abroad, even if it was in a secular job. You could also ask someone who has been on holiday somewhere unusual to speak about their experiences.

Videos often go down well. You could choose either one produced by a missionary society, or a tape of a relevant TV programme.

Organise finance-raising events or find other projects which the members can work at together and which will benefit people based in other countries, such as crocheting blankets or knitting simple garments for children.

Arrange a bring-and-share meal with an international flavour, encouraging members who come from other ethnic backgrounds to bring tasters of their national dishes. This will help them to feel valued and accepted. Invite them to talk about their cultural background and experiences too.

Ladies can also be encouraged to support local meetings associated with the Womans World Day of Prayer, the liturgy for which is prepared by women from a different country each year.

Input for men

How about serving up an exotic breakfast of tropical fruits next time the men meet for a prayer breakfast, or adding a mission prayer bookmark or country profile to the place settings?

The men could be encouraged to organise a collection day for unwanted household and garden tools in reasonable condition on behalf of one of the agencies who send these overseas. (See section IV of the Directory at the back of this book).

There are lots of practical ways in which men (and women with the appropriate strength or skills) can help you: making a new display board or repositioning the old one; moving the furniture around for a special mission event; chauffeuring people to events; building sets and sorting out props for drama presentations; being responsible for the technical side of arranging a live telephone link.

Homegroups

These are a strategic base for increasing the number of people involved in world-mission support. Each group can be encouraged to adopt specific individuals, people groups, sending agencies, and to focus their praying, giving, letter-writing and news-sharing on these.

Then they could be asked to share in the church's education programme, taking turns to give a five minute news-update during the Sunday service, to write a brief report for the news-sheet or Parish magazine, or to mount a topical display or organise a special event.

You could also try some of the study materials which are available on the theme of world-mission and are particularly suited to use in small informal groups.

Children's work

This subject is dealt with in depth in Chapter 7.

Well-informed people become more effective pray-ers

The aim of all this information-sharing is to help people progress beyond the occasional vague prayers which are just a dipping of the toe into the shallows of a vast ocean. The small numbers who turn out for any prayer meeting, let alone a missionary one, indicate that these have a reputation for being boring, when quite the reverse can be true! Surely the formal format often adopted for such meetings is responsible for this.

Prayer is the most important aspect of world-mission support and is what every overseas Christian worker relies on. It is the only activity which is not subject to the physical limitations imposed by geographical distance, health, politics, financial situation, or the busy schedules and other responsibilities which tie us down. Michael Griffiths writes: 'Prayer enables us to participate in Christian work taking place thousands of miles away, in places we have never been to in the past, or will never visit in the future.' [3]

What could be more exciting or worthwhile than that?

Making prayer for mission part of every group's thinking

It takes time and effort to lead a church into experiencing this tremendous privilege to the full. Once world-mission has begun to be part of people's thinking, the next step is to bring prayer for mission out of the confines of small specialised midweek groups attended by the already committed core, and into the intercessions of other meetings on a regular basis.

Making the needs known

Prayer goes hand-in-hand with information-sharing which is varied, stimulating and dispersed in manageable amounts. We all learn better through finding out, doing and thinking, rather than merely sitting and listening.

Since praying is such an important part of mission support, how about appointing one member of your mission action-group to be responsible for collating and communicating information for prayer?

Involving those who cannot get to meetings

Prayer tapes are especially useful for those who find it difficult to get out to meetings. Tapes can be copied and circulated to the elderly, the housebound, the visually impaired, the young parent.

Commuters can listen to them on their way to work.

Sharing information to fuel prayer

● *The notice-board*

A small, easily portable notice-board displaying quarterly calendar-style prayer bulletins from the societies linked with the church is an excellent way to remind people of the wider world. This could be taken to any regular prayer meeting.

Another helpful approach is to devote a small area of the main missionary display-board to current world needs, so that people will begin to link the news headlines with prayer. The display could be updated weekly or fort-nightly as appropriate.

● *The church magazine*

Magazine editors often welcome extracts from missionary letters or maga-zines to print in the newsletter or parish magazine. A precis of prayer requests could also be included.

● *Prayer aids*

Advertise regularly the many materials produced to help us in our praying: calendars, diaries, letters, bulletins, up-dates on the Internet for those soci-eties with Web-sites, numbers to phone for recorded prayer requests.

● *Missionary magazines*

Missionary magazines are an excellent way of keeping up to date with current news and issues. Why not order back numbers to give away to prospective readers as they come into the church, to show them what they are missing! Alternatively use your Sunday mission slot for some imaginative advertising.

● *Prayer letters*

These can be used at meetings or circulated amongst individuals for private use.

Though some prayer letters are easy to read, others are very wordy or hard to understand, especially if they are full of unexplained abbreviations, initials and obscure references. Produce an edited version containing a precis of the main points, preferably set out in bulleted paragraphs. One copy can be dis-played on the world-mission board, and the rest handed to people as they arrive or leave.

Another way to involve those who are shut in is by organising a prayer chain for phoning around urgent prayer requests from your missionaries.

Alternative ideas for prayer meetings

The traditional option is to sit everyone in a group and then play them a tape, a video, or read out a letter or bulletin, following this with one long session of open prayer. Such meetings are ineffective for two reasons. Firstly, little of the content will be remembered simply because the attention-span of most people is limited when just sitting and listening. Secondly, a formal, predictable format is unlikely to attract newcomers, especially younger people.

Ring the changes with some of the following ideas:

- Tape brief extracts from secular TV or radio programmes featuring the countries you are linked with through missionaries or societies. Natural history programmes often convey useful information about climate, terrain and the general environment which helps to build a more comprehensive picture of the context in which your missionaries live and work. Short focused sessions, in which you play a snippet of tape, then pray, play another clip and pray again, can work well especially if people are tired at the end of a demanding day.

- For a more energetic session, confront supporters with examples of dilemmas which frequently face overseas workers. Role-playing exercises and discussion materials are available which encourage participants to consider what they would do in given circumstances and thereby discover how difficult making the 'right' decision can be. This helps develop their praying beyond simply counting off the points listed at the end of a letter, to imagining how they would feel if they were 'X' and converting this into prayer.

- To encourage everyone to join in, however shy, make cards from thin cardboard onto which are glued pictures or snippets from missionary magazines. Each person takes a card and spends five minutes silently praying for that subject. Afterwards some might be encouraged to talk about the thoughts which the card has inspired in them. The cards are then swapped around and the group divided into pairs or threesomes. For five minutes these pairs share and pray together. Finally everyone is brought back together and all the cards placed on a poster map of the world for a final ten-minute session of open prayer, still focusing on these. It is surprising how fast an hour will pass.

● Instead of listening to a cassette or watching a video, how about making one to send to the missionaries for whom you pray? Check first that the recipients have the equipment to play it. Your tape does not have to be super-spiritual. Missionaries will enjoy listening to ordinary news, every-day happenings in your church and community, some of your chatting together, and even part of your prayer-time. What an encouragement, to hear you actually praying for them. Added to which, as they learn about you they can pray for you too. Now that is partnership!

Making it personal

So much for information-sharing and prayer. What really gets a church launched into world-mission is that personal link with somebody they know and care about: someone from their own number who has responded to God's call to overseas work, or a visitor with whom the group has built up a friendship. 'There is nothing like having a member of your congregation leave for the mission field to stir people up.'[4]

The next stage of building a strong mission-support framework is to plan how to strengthen such a link to the mutual benefit of both supporters and supported.

Further reading

Creating World Mission Awareness (Administry's Adminisheet 54).

Michael Griffiths, A Task Unfinished (Monarch, 1996).

Patrick Johnstone, The Church is Bigger than you Think (Christian Focus Publishing/ WEC, 1998).

Glenn Myers, The World Christian Starter Kit (WEC Publications, 1993).

Footnotes

1 From Your Church and the World (Administry Resource paper 83:3, copyright Administry 1983). Quoted with permission.

2 Rev. Fred Stainthorpe, 'Open Line: World-mission Focus' (Baptist Times, 24th November 1994). Used with permission.

3 A Task Unfinished p.115.

4 Malcolm Widdecombe in Michael Griffiths (ed.), Ten Sending Churches, p.33.

Summary of resources

Courses (see section II of the Directory at the end of this book for addresses).

- *Culture to Culture,* St. John's Extension Studies. An open-learning course in cross-cultural mission: 5 modules, including The World Christian; Issues in Mission Today; Entering Another's World. (Initial enquiry advised).
- Details of other courses on mission, including correspondence courses which vary from a few days duration to two or three years, can be found in *The Training Directory,* available from Christian Vocations .
- *The UK Christian Handbook Millenium Edition* (Christian Research/ Harper Collins Religious, 1999), has comprehensive lists of training centres and courses.
- YWAM publish a directory of their own courses.

Prayer aids for individuals
- Prayer guides, diaries, calendars. (send an SAE to individual societies for their catalogues).

Prayer guides and information
- *Intercessors Worldwide.* A quarterly summary sheet of news from around the world. (Details from WEC International).
- *Newsbytes* (OM News and Information). A roundup of world religious news compiled monthly which may be freely copied and circulated. For a free e-mail subscription write: <majordomo@om.org> In the message line type: subscribe newsbytes.
- Patrick Johnstone, *Operation World* (WEC, 1993).
- Prayer card packs: (OM Publishing).
- Tearline: 0208 977 2079. For up to date news and prayer requests.
- *World Prayer News* (Global Connections). A bimonthly compendium.

Resource packs for group use
- *Church Starter Pack* (AIM).
- *Planting for the future* (Interserve). A prayer-pack for house-groups.
- *Power Pack Pages* (BMS).
- *Why Bother with Mission?* (IVP, 1996). A church starter pack which includes the book of the same title, by Steve Gaukroger, plus study guides and video. Available from IVP.

3

Missionaries are human too

Support for individual missionaries

'I feel as if I'm being swept under the carpet,' said one missionary sadly, when asked how she was treated during home-leave. 'People don't want to know.'

'Most people develop a glazed look in their eyes after five minutes,' said another. 'We have just learned to accept that what they really want to do is talk about themselves, rather than listen to us.'

Despite the large amount of literature available on how to support missionaries, and despite the sending societies' increasing efforts to share responsibility for missionaries with the churches, many missionaries still feel like second-class citizens. This particularly applies to link missionaries who are adopted by churches to whom they are complete strangers.

Sadly, however, it may even be true of those who go out from a church's own membership. The passing of time, and the geographical and cultural distance between missionary and supporters can all too easily dampen the latter's initial enthusiasm and good intentions.

On the other hand, many missionaries do feel loved and supported, and thank God continually for the encouragement and help they receive from their link churches.

So what makes the difference? Much depends on how great an investment of time and energy a church is prepared to devote to building and maintaining the relationship between home-base and missionaries. Offering meaningful support to someone whose work-place is a world away from your own does not come easily. It is hard to get going but the process will gather momentum once you are on your way.

Realising missionaries are human

Few missionaries want to be put on a pedestal. They know all too well that they have not suddenly been transformed into a super-human angelic life-form, and despite their label they, like all of us, need care and prayer.

Anne Townsend encourages us to be practical: 'Never feel that your missionary is so spiritual and so perfect that he doesn't need the ordinary kind of pastoring that other sheep in God's flock need. If you think that way, you delude yourself! Your missionary has spiritual needs, deficiencies and strengths in the same way that each member of the body of Christ has them.[1] In recognising this, we engage our imaginations and try to put ourselves in our missionaries' shoes.

Discovering where they are at

Although you will never be able to know completely what life is like for your missionaries unless you become one yourself, you can learn a lot if you are prepared to listen carefully both to what your own missionaries say and to what others share through tapes, talks and the written word.

Many helpful books are available and reading these is as good a place to start as any (see the Recommended Reading section at the end of the chapter). Relevant articles may also be found in missionary magazines.

Books written by or for missionaries can be as useful as those written specifically to advise supporters. They often contain enlightening passages. In *Who'd be a Missionary?* Helen Morgan describes how, on arriving at her new post abroad, she felt 'a mad urge to run anywhere, as long as it was away from where strangers waited to turn the key of my future prison'.[2]

In *Prepared to Serve* Eva recalls feeling 'as new and vulnerable as a baby. I could not even communicate basic things like 'hello' in the appropriate way. I had to learn how to eat, how to behave, what to wear. And like a baby I got very tired by all these new experiences, especially with learning the language, and I found I could not cope with as much as I expected.'[3]

Cathy, another short-term volunteer, writes of her first impression of the country she went to:

> . . . No amount of reading, talking to people, seeing slides or photos could have prepared me for the 'baptism' that was to ensue as I stepped from the heavenly detachment of the plane flight: overwhelming mugginess that clothes you with its steamy heat; smells of burning charcoal, car exhausts, open sewage, body heat; explosions of colour in clothes, flowers, painted vehicles; the throb of people everywhere; the noise of the city, crickets and frogs at night, voodoo drums, death wails ... I felt guilty, angry and frustrated. I had winged my way from reading, preparation, an orientation course, a myriad vaccinations, and an exciting and expectant farewell service at my home church which emphasised 'sending out for service in the Third-World'. Now I was looking into the face of the 'Third-World' in utter helplessness.[4]

Visiting missionaries

One way to identify with your missionaries and to offer them pastoral care is to visit them once they have had time to settle in. This shows you are willing to expose yourselves to the culture shock and the change of environment which they have had to face and to share their experiences. True empathy is often the by-product of personal experience.

Some points to consider

Not every missionary is in a position to receive a visit, or would welcome one. It depends on their personality and the demands of their schedules.

Missionaries who expressed enthusiasm to me for the idea (most who were asked), did so with the proviso that churches consult them throughout the planning process, and think prayerfully about the kind of people selected to make the

Wendy gazed out of the window in awe at the magnificent mountain scenery below, as the plane approached its destination. It would not be long before they landed and she would arrive in Nepal at last. She could hardly believe it.

An enthusiastic supporter of missionaries for years, eighty-year-old Wendy returned from her one-month trip even more fired-up and all the better equipped to enthuse others with vibrant accounts of her own experiences and observations.

Henry and Molly decided to visit Martine, the missionary they prayed for regularly, and to take some video footage of their prayer group to her in the Philippines. They wanted her to see her supporters and hear some of their prayers for herself. Whilst there they made a video for the prayer group featuring Martine in her place of work, so that they too could share in the visit, 'meet' Martine and her colleagues and see her home. This made their partnership with her all the more personal and real. The video they made of Martine was also useful for her to borrow and show other supporters during her next home-leave.

visit. Such a visit demands a great deal from the missionary. Although intended to make them feel loved and supported, it can result in their feeling stressed out, especially if they feel under pressure to put on a good show and be a super-spiritual hero, living a life of constant victory and never losing their cool. Making sure visitors are well prepared and aware they are visiting an ordinary human being will help guard against this danger.

It is also important to choose visitors who will be sensitive to their host's needs and situation; people who are adaptable and have initiative, and are unlikely to get under their host's feet. They should be able to report back to the rest of the church in a way which grabs their listeners' interest, spurring them on to pray with greater understanding, and to offer more appropriate practical support. This, after all, is the main purpose of such a visit.

Visitors can act as couriers, transporting gifts and useful items which could not be posted easily, so it helps if they are prepared to limit their personal luggage to the bare essentials.

A personal visit not only encourages missionaries to feel they really do matter, it can also be a powerful means of recruiting new supporters and volunteers, as people see the realities of a missionary's work situation, experience worship in a foreign language and culture, eat different food, find out there is more than one way to do things, and face the suffering and poverty first-hand. All this has the potential for making a unique impact on your church, especially when those who make the visit are from the church's leadership team.

Counting the cost

Offering long-term, meaningful support is costly. It is costly in terms of energy-expenditure. It is hard work keeping up the impetus of that initial enthusiasm. It may even take considerable effort to arouse any real interest in the first place.

It is costly in financial terms. Money is needed to send letters and parcels; make phone calls; visit; offer accommodation, transport, new clothes, household items, or even a holiday, when missionaries are on home-leave.

It is costly in terms of the time and effort needed to keep in touch, to find out what is needed or wanted and make time regularly for prayer.

It is costly in terms of discouragement. There will be times when you have tried so hard but to little avail. People let you down. The theory sounded good but does not seem to be working out in practice. Maybe your aspirations were too ambitious, or did not get the response you had hoped for. It is sorely tempting to give up when people lose interest.

It is costly in terms of patience. If you are not careful, your own enthusiasm may leave other people behind. It is tempting to try to do everything at once. However, it is more realistic to concentrate on the following essentials which every missionary values most. You can always build on these later as appropriate.

Foundation stones

Pray regularly. Write regularly. This is the starting point. Everyone knows how important it is to be prayed for and how good it is to receive something in the post, even a simple postcard saying 'Wish you were here!'

In churches linked with more than one missionary, responsibility for keeping in touch with them and passing on their news can be shared amongst the home groups or church organisations to encourage as many people as possible to be involved.

Prayer

The first essential is regular specific prayer: for health, protection, wisdom, and provision for every need, physically, spiritually and emotionally. OMF's pamphlet *How to pray for missionaries* is well worth adding to your stock.

You can never spend too much time encouraging people to pray: regularly, corporately, privately, even impulsively. Countless missionaries testify to occasions which have been completely turned around because someone, somewhere, responded to God's prompting and without knowing the details of why or what for, prayed for them.

Letters

Letters are a lifeline. They are essential number two, providing a tangible link with home and reassuring your missionaries that they have not been forgotten.

When Helen Tett and her husband first went out to Africa as missionaries just

---

Here are some guidelines to help you make the most of your letters.

● Write regularly, not just during your missionaries' early days but throughout their term abroad.

● Do not be discouraged if letters are not answered quickly. Missionaries are very busy people, and sometimes mail goes astray.

● Letters do not have to be sermon synopses, neither do they have to be very long. Encourage people to write everyday news, jokes and funny stories, remembering that a good laugh can be a great healer in the middle of frustration and loneliness.

● Picture postcards are also appreciated. Once read they can be kept as reminders of home.

● Birthday cards and Christmas cards are important too. You could even tuck a couple of blank cards inside these for the missionary to use for other people.

● Providing each organisation in the church in turn with an air letter for all the members to write their own short messages means that everyone eventually gets involved, rather than just the dedicated letter-writers who tend to be a rarity nowadays.

● *If your missionaries are based in a politically sensitive country, make sure letter-writers are given a copy of any guidelines available and are made aware of how important it is to keep to these.*

after the Second World War, their mail took up to a week to arrive from the nearest collection point 100 miles away. The safe arrival of the letters was greeted with excitement, however much they smelt of the kerosene transported with them, which often spilled onto them making them partly illegible.

Today's missionaries welcome letters just as eagerly.

E-mail

Written communication is no longer restricted to the postal system. More and more missionaries have access to equipment which enables the exchange of e-mails and faxes. These are as immediate as a phone-call but have the advantage of generally being both versatile and cheap. They are especially useful if your missionaries request copies of documents or pictures, or need information urgently. However, some countries operate restrictions or make additional charges for specific Internet service providers, so check if the recipient is likely to be charged before encouraging people to send them e-mails, especially before sending large files.

Building on the foundation

There is always more to be done.

When thinking about how to expand the practical support you give to your missionaries as a church, encourage people to imagine what they would appreciate if they were in the missionaries' situation. What would they miss most? What would they find difficult to cope with?

Missionary Bob missed brown sauce. His wife Sue liked to receive catalogues so that she could keep up to date with fashions, and appreciated paperbacks for leisure reading. Helen eagerly looks forward to Christmas, when she knows she will get a parcel containing a novel from one of her supporters.

Knowing what your missionaries would like depends on how well you know them and how comfortable they feel about telling you their individual needs and wants. You may have to amend and update your basic list at regular intervals as their requirements change over the years.

A missionary's needs are sometimes unpredictable. But God knows their needs and may prompt his people to act in specific but at the time unaccountable ways. Missionary Mary Cundy could hardly believe her eyes when she opened a parcel from her eight-year-old god-daughter. Because she was one of just three Commonwealth citizens based in Nepal at that time, Mary had received an invi-

---

What would your missionary like?

Here are some suggestions:

- Packet soup or a casserole mix: a plain meal can be transformed by adding one of these.

- Dessert mixes are useful too, and everyone seems to crave chocolate!

- Tapes of secular music, a selection of new worship songs, a comedy classic or fiction cassette, can provide welcome relaxation.

- Plasters, pens, sticky tape and notepaper. Many ordinary things may be unobtainable and are sadly missed. Even the packaging in which gifts arrive may be useful and recycled.

- Magazines to help them keep up to date with hobbies, trends, news, special interests. Printed paper rate enables favourite magazines and newspapers, national and local, to be sent reasonably cheaply, and these can matter a lot to people based overseas.

---

tation to go to Pokhara (three day's trek away) to be presented to the Queen. Protocol was still strictly observed in those days and a hat and white gloves had to worn for such occasions: not standard missionary garb and certainly not readily available in Nepal. So imagine how excited Mary felt when she discovered that the parcel (posted six months previously) contained a pair of white gloves which fitted perfectly and matched her one and only hat![5]

Unfortunately not every package can be guaranteed to arrive safely. Parcels can be a particular temptation as their contents usually have to be listed on the outside, so increasing the risk of their being tampered with. Envelopes may be less risky, as long as these are not too heavy to send letter-rate. Small items such as the odd sachet of instant hot-chocolate, a few teabags flattened and wrapped in plastic, elastic bands, a pretty hair-fastener, a newspaper article, a couple of photographs of church family events, can be tucked inside a letter or card.

Guidelines for posting items abroad can be obtained from your local Post Office. Check relevant customs regulations with your missionaries so they do not end up having to pay heavy customs duties on what you have sent.

Appointing a mailing co-ordinator from the mission action-group to oversee this aspect of support would probably be helpful. A clearly labelled collection point with a list of suitable items displayed alongside provides a permanent site where people can safely leave their contributions.

Catering for 'mish-kids'

Encourage the children at church to become penfriends with missionaries' children.

They could send small, lightweight collectibles such as the free gifts from cereal packets. Books, comics, travel games, story tapes and selections of pop music would also be appreciated. Children coming home from abroad who have not heard of the latest groups and fashions, which matter right from early primary school nowadays, are at a severe disadvantage and at risk of being marginalised or bullied by their peers. Keeping 'mish-kids' in touch with their own culture would be a really valuable way of involving the younger members of your church.

Caring for missionaries' relatives and friends

Have you considered the possibility of extending the pastoral care you show your missionaries to include members of their families who remain in this country, assuming that links can be made with them naturally and without seeming to intrude? Even the committed Christians, whom you may blithely assume are rejoicing in the fact that their loved ones are 'serving the Lord', feel bereft and probably have a good cry at times. Ageing or worried parents, unchurched relatives, children at senior school, college or university, brothers, sisters, close friends, also need your loving prayers and sensitive support.

Helen and Charles Tett, working in Africa, felt indebted to those who acted as substitute parents for their children when they reached the stage of having to be educated in the UK. Another missionary, Diane, thanked God for a ninety-year-old lady who kept in touch faithfully with her mum, reassuring *her* and sharing news with her.

Caring for your missionaries when they come home

Practical and pastoral care are also essential when your missionaries return for home-leave or for good.

Even experienced long-term missionaries find it hard to keep up with the rapid pace of change at home. Each time they return some new gadget has become essential: microwave ovens, video recorders, personal computers, mobile phones, supermarket reward cards. So much can change even in the space of a few months. New shopping centres spring up, a one-way system is totally re-organised, food scares and dietary fashions mean certain foods may no longer be available, and words change their meaning.

Reverse culture-shock is often more traumatic than the shock experienced on entering another country. Keeping your missionaries up to date with what is happening in everyday life goes some way towards preparing them for their homecoming. Giving them plenty of time to adjust when they return is also very important, even though it is tempting to expect them to slot in straight away. It is vital to listen to them, so that we can be sensitive to their needs and help them rather than unintentionally adding to the pressure they are under. Their families and friends who remained at home may also find this period of adjustment difficult and need your support too.

Some practical suggestions

A 'missionary shower' can be a real blessing. Your missionaries' safe return is an occasion to celebrate, so how about holding a party, once they have had time to settle down? You could invite people to bring presents or gift vouchers to express their continuing love and support and at the same time provide those everyday essentials which missionaries rarely have in stock on their immediate return: household cleaning materials, stationery, toiletries, games and toys for the children, magazines, basic medicines, fashionable clothes and footwear, pretty bedlinen, soft towels, radio and TV listings, tapes, postage stamps. How about including a few treats, like tickets for a film, concert or play, and money for a meal out, a takeaway, or a new hair-do?

Make sure the food cupboard in their house is well stocked with goodies *before* they arrive and that basic utensils such as saucepans and tin-openers are available.

Offering the loan of a car (in working order and with a tankful of petrol), or ensuring that the central heating in the furlough house is efficient and the washing machine is not about to break down, are all ways of showing your missionaries that you regard them as being worth the very best you can offer.

In her book *Faith without Pretending,* Anne Townsend recalls the shower-party held for her family by the local church.

'I felt young and bridal again as we were deluged with what seemed like wedding presents all over again - the things which had been destroyed and worn out in the tropics were replaced with beautiful brand new gifts. For me, an ex-missionary, receiving so many new beautiful things was a laughter-making and tear-making experience. I was used to the second-hand, the nearly-new and the cast-offs and had not realised how much I yearned for new things until this church lavished gifts on us. Somehow I had allowed myself to feel that I was only a second-hand person along with my second-hand clothes. I began to taste the joy of feeling I was worth more than I had realised in the past, and that was a gift beyond price from that church.'[6]

Your consistent prayerful support and loving care will help your missionaries to feel they really are part of your church family, and at the same time it will make you feel an important part of what they are doing. Surely this is a privilege and a unique opportunity not to be missed, and well worth all the effort.

Footnotes

1   *Love your local Missionary*, p.51.
2   *Who'd be a missionary*, p.4.
3   Derek Williams (ed.), *Prepared to serve*, p.50.
4   *Ibid*, p.62.
5   Mary Cundy, *Better than the Witchdoctor*, p.277.
6   p.82-83, quoted with the author's permission.

Further reading

Some of the following may be out of print. However, you may be able to track them down in second-hand book shops or Christian libraries. Alternatively, you could contact Book Aid (address in section VI of the Directory). American publications may be ordered from Christian bookshops, borrowed from specialist libraries, or ordered from overseas stockists via the Internet.

Personal accounts of living and travelling overseas

Mary Cundy, *Better than the Witchdoctor* (Monarch, 1994).

Elizabeth Goldsmith, Roots and Wings: *Five generations and their influence* (OM Publishing, 1998).

Martin Goldsmith, *Life's Tapestry* (OM Publishing, 1999).

Helen Morgan, *Who'd be a Missionary?* (Patmos, 1965).

———————— *Who'd Stay a Missionary?* (Patmos, 1971).

Stephen Rand, *Guinea Pig for Lunch* (Hodder and Stoughton, 1998).

How to support your missionaries

Stephen Gaukroger, *Why Bother with Mission?* (IVP, 1996).

Martin Goldsmith (ed.), *Love your local Missionary* (Marc, 1984).

Michael Griffiths, *A Task Unfinished* (Monarch, 1996).

———————— *Get your Church Involved in Missions!* (OMF Books, 1972).

Neal Pirolo, *Serving as Senders : How to care for your missionaries* (OM Publishing, 1997).

Fiction based on fact

Rhena Taylor, *Rough Edges* (IVP, 1978).

———————— *The Prisoner* (Marc, 1987).

Guidelines for missionaries

Ian and Jean Gately, *My Reasonable Service?* (Pentland Press, 1995).

Elizabeth Goldsmith, *Getting from there to here* (OM Publishing, rev. edn 1995).

Peter Jordan, *Re-entry: Making the transition from missions to life at home* (YWAM Publishing, 1992).

Betty Jo Kennedy, *The Missionary Family* (William Carey Library, 1983).

Kelly O'Donnell, *Missionary Care: Counting the cost for world evangelisation* (William Carey Library, 1992).

Derek Williams (ed.), *Prepared to serve* (Tearfund/SU: 1989).

Booklets

How to pray for missionaries (OMF).

Now that I'm Home (OM).

What can I do? A manual for making the most of your missionary, (Wycliffe Bible Translators, 1999).

4

No special talent required

Making good displays

There it stands at the back of the church, tatty and unnoticed, the mission notice-board. Though often regarded as an essential part of the decor, showing at least some awareness of Christ's great commission in Matthew 28, it looks sadly neglected. The world map in the centre is fading in places, and the missionary photographs pinned alongside are too small to see from any distance. The poster at the other side is crinkled and out of date and a yellowing prayer letter dangles listlessly from the bottom corner. It is so long since the display was last changed that nobody sees it anymore, let alone stops to read it. It is certainly no match for the slick publicity which continually bombards us from every side.

To be effective, the world mission notice-board desperately needs a greater investment of time and effort than has been given to it in the past. A well-designed, interesting display can stimulate and enthuse people, even those who would not necessarily go to a missionary meeting. It may inspire prayer and giving, and may even provide the initial challenge which eventually leads someone to volunteer for service.

In this chapter we will look first at the importance of getting the contents right and then at the practicalities of how to put it all together.

Choosing your topics

'Our missionaries'

If you have only one display board, you will probablyòbe required to allocate at least some of this space to information about your church's missionaries. Though fairly static by nature, the display can be changed around regularly and updated to keep people looking. Space could be set aside for recent prayer requests, and the addition of the occasional map, country profile or photograph of your missionaries 'in action' will ensure the display remains interesting. Material may also be retrieved from articles written by or about your missionaries or the area in which they serve, either in missionary magazines or secular publications such as national newspapers. Obtaining duplicate copies makes it easier to display both sides of a page, though in the case of long passages of small print it may be better to select just a few extracts to cut out and mount on card.

Wider issues

Whilst it is vital to use the display area for sustaining people's interest in their link missionaries, it is also important to use some of the space for stimulating a deeper level of world-awareness, raising wider issues. A selection of basic facts about the country, person or situation you are spotlighting can be printed out separately on plain postcards or index cards. *Operation World* is an indispensable source of basic information. Selected details or biographical notes about workers can help flesh out the picture for their supporters, hopefully resulting in a increased level of understanding and interest.

The setting out of several identical or different sized copies of a poster, symmetrically or in some other pattern, can also be eye-catching.

If you can have only one board, either set aside a corner for these topics or explore the possibility of having the occasional table-top display in front of the board.

Creating world awareness does not have to be heavy-going. In fact, humour can be useful too! The *Pontius Puddle* cartoons from Tearfund's *Tear Times* are a good example of thought-provoking fun.

The element of surprise or shock on a display can be very effective, for example by juxtaposing pictures of everyday situations from different cultures: a busy motorway and an empty rutted track: a ragged, malnourished child in a refugee camp and a smartly clothed Western child tucking into a chocolate bar.

Focusing on specifics

Concentrating on a specific theme, month by month, will enable people to assimilate information about world-mission in manageable amounts. Ideas for topical themes can be gleaned from missionary magazines and newspaper headlines, or inspired by occasions designated nationally or worldwide to highlight issues like Aids. Focusing on current concerns helps people to make links between events going on in the world and their implications for world-mission.

Ideas for themes and titles

- *A Tale of Two Cities:* a display featuring two contrasting capital cities.
- *Homelessness around the world.*
- *Thank God for these things:* pictures of positive examples of front-line projects which are making a difference.
- *Mountain states:* pictures of mountainous countries.
- *Our Asian Neighbours:* examples of what is being done to reach ethnic minorities in this country.
- *Prisoners of conscience:* around the world.
- *Sharing the darkness:* scenes of people coming alongside and helping those in difficulty, both in this country and abroad.
- *Faces of the family:* a collection of pictures of families around the world.
- *On the move:* different modes of transport, focusing on the work of Mission Aviation Fellowship in particular.
- *Faces behind the headlines or trouble spots* – featuring situations in the news.[1]

Human interest

People have an insatiable interest in other people, hence the appeal of 'fly-on-the-wall' real life documentaries. Exploit this natural curiosity by featuring aspects of everyday life such as food, education or employment.

Bringing your display-board to life

Enlisting help

The task will be a lot easier if you find people with the necessary skills and resources to help you. Many children and young people are both competent and highly motivated when it comes to using computers for graphics and design. Enlisting their help, especially if they have access to a home computer and colour printer suitable for desktop publishing, is a possibility well worth exploring. They will be able to produce posters and illustrated news bulletins professionally and relatively cheaply, and since most churches now have photocopiers, black and white copies can also be made without too much expense. If you know people, of any age, who have a flair for art and design, or love playing around on a computer, why not invite them onto your team? This will not only ease your load but may also stimulate their interest in world-mission.

However, producing displays may well be left largely in your own hands. This may be a daunting prospect, particularly if you are not very artistic. Some basic guidelines will help make your board as effective as possible.

Gathering resources

Recently I spent an exhilarating day with one mission co-ordinator with a truly missionary zeal for creating displays for her board. She spent time every evening searching her daily paper for photographs, headlines and other materials which could come in useful. This level of activity would not be possible for everyone, but the basic principle of being on the lookout for anything which could be useful pays dividends. It provides a good stock-pile on which to draw, so that when you get round to putting a display together, you have plenty of material already available, rather than having to start from scratch.

A sizeable stock of materials can be accumulated at little or no cost and stored in document wallets. These can be labelled clearly according to country, continent, topic or society so relevant material is easy to retrieve.

Missionary magazines are particularly fertile ground. Good quality photographs, pictures, maps, cartoons, titles and headings can all be cut out and kept along with any articles which will not date quickly. Graphs or statistics can also be useful, as long as they are dated clearly so they can be discarded when no longer relevant.

Articles and photographs in secular magazines and travel brochures are another good source of background information about everyday aspects of life abroad which often interest people – landscapes, markets, shops, houses, transport, wildlife, work, play, and so on.

One pastor recommends sending off to Embassies of different countries for good quality background material.

A large selection of pictures, maps, flags and cartoons, along with a wide range of fonts for lettering is readily available on Clip Art CDs, both Christian and secular. Encyclopaedias are also available on CD. These are useful sources of maps, facts and figures, photographs and illustrations which can be printed out.

Building up a good basic stock of stationery materials is also important: rulers, gluesticks, felt-tipped and highlighter pens, and so on. A plentiful supply of coloured card is useful. However, shelf-paper, recycled packing card, or the plain backs of used posters provide adequate backgrounds on which to mount smaller items and are much cheaper than sheets of card.

Positioning

A board tucked away in a hallway or dark corner has no chance of making any impact. Think about where people stand before and after meetings in your church. Do they tend to congregate in the foyer, or a lounge or side-room? Where does their gaze rest while they sit waiting for the service to start or while the offering is taken up?

In the light of all this, where would be the most strategic place to position your notice-board? Is it best to place the board in a permanent position, or would a light-weight portable board be a better option?

Many mission boards are hung too high for children to see. Why not include something specifically for children, such as a puzzle, word search, or some other brain-teaser displayed at their eye-level? Children relish a chance to prove how clever they are, and a small prize for those who manage to work out the answer will provide an extra incentive. Children could also be invited to help by making collages on a mission theme using magazine pictures, or by colouring in headings, pictures or flags for your display.

Arranging a three-dimensional display once in a while is worth considering, especially for special events. Several different levels can easily be achieved by placing firm cardboard boxes of various heights and sizes onto a table top and then covering them with a plain sheet or tablecloth. A number of open books, artefacts, everyday objects from another country or fair-trade products can then be displayed even if the space available is limited.

Planning

Time spent on careful planning is never wasted. However original your ideas and eye-catching your materials, the way in which they are assembled and presented is vital if they are to achieve maximum visibility. It is easy to bombard people with a chaotic mass of colour and information. 'Bold' is not necessarily 'best'. You may stop people in their tracks, but it is doubtful whether they will take in much of such a dazzling conglomeration, and they will probably only look once. Simplicity is very effective but can be surprisingly difficult to achieve; it requires careful planning.

Once you have chosen your theme, relevant material can be retrieved from your stockpile. Choose the pieces you want, taking care to keep a balance between written and pictorial content. The ideal is to have a maximum of one third written material to two thirds pictorial.

Lettering

Important phrases or brief quotations can be highlighted or reproduced from any articles which you decide to display.

Mount titles on plain card, taking care that any hand-written ones are large enough to read at a distance. Drawing the lettering out in pencil first helps to space it evenly, and the guidelines can be rubbed out later. Choose bright, strong colours for lettering, outlined in black.

Computers are a huge advantage here, with all the choices of font, size, borders and shading now available.

Large letters made from coloured card can be bought from some toy shops and are useful for a main heading if you have not got much spare time. Multi-coloured magnetic letters, also from toy departments, can be attached to the board with loops of sticky tape or Blu-tack. Stencils, transfers, cut-outs and tracing paper are easy alternatives for producing lettering with a professional look if you do not have a steady hand.

Mounting your materials

Pastel coloured backing-paper is a good foil to a display of big, bright pictures and posters. Pictures, photographs and extracts from articles can be mounted on neutral-coloured, suitably sized cards. Brightly coloured mounts tend to distract from the information displayed on them. Related information can be mounted on the same colour card, to make it easy to see what relates to what.

Mounting small items together on large pieces of paper to create posters or montages is more effective visually than mounting them individually, although some items may be kept aside for filling awkward spaces. Using a variety of shapes and sizes adds to the visual interest as long as they are carefully arranged in a balanced pattern and have reasonably straight edges.

Positioning individual items on the background and making a faint pencil mark at each corner will help you remember where to fix them when you are ready to do so.

Assembling your display

When everything is ready, either lay the board down on a flat surface, or else find a table-top of comparable size on which you can experiment with how to arrange the various items. If the board is wall-mounted, fix items with a minimum number of pins until you are satisfied with the effect.

Starting at the outer edges of the board and working inwards helps to space the items evenly. Designate one item as your eye-catcher, which can then be placed anywhere with everything else arranged neatly around it.

Map pins with small beaded tops blend in much better than ordinary drawing pins, especially if colour matched to their background. They are also easier to remove afterwards.

If you find an individual item still does not show up well even when mounted on a plain background, try drawing a simple frame around it in black with pen and ruler as this can make a noticeable difference.

Other places to go for help

There are many sources of help and inspiration around. It can be very useful to talk to people who have to put displays together as part of their job, such as teachers, librarians, shop-keepers and museum curators. There may be techniques which you could adapt for your notice-board. Similarly, when visiting other churches, if their mission boards catch your eye try to work out why.

Your library may have helpful books about display techniques in the education, design and business sections.

By being prepared to experiment and to learn by trial and error you will broaden your scope and find out what works best in your situation.

You can do it!

It may not be easy to attract people's attention in a world where we are continually being targeted by eye-catching advertisements and professionally designed window-displays, but it is still possible for the imaginative and dedicated to make a successful visual impact with their mission board.

All the planning, cutting, gluing and pinning involved may even cease to be a chore and become a challenge and a joy, if people's interest in mission increases as a result of your efforts.

Resource materials:

A1 flexible display panel available for purchase from CMS. (This comes with an excellent collection of advice sheets, suggested layouts, and headings which can be photocopied for display purposes.)

A4 mounted table-top displays can be borrowed from BMS.

Christian Clip Art images on CD available from Sunrise Software and Christian Computer Art. Or visit the Free Christian Software Directory web-site (with other links to graphics) at http://www.seriousd.com/clipart.htm

Country profiles, maps and posters available from individual missionary organisations. Some examples are:
- Elim International Missions: fact-file/country sheets and a display list of laminated photos.
- Global Connections: set of eye-catching posters, each covering a region or people group.
- Interserve: country leaflets and world map.
- Leprosy Mission: posters and large World Leprosy Map.
- Tearfund: themed posters.
- Wycliffe Bible Translators: posters and people profiles.

Laminated display pictures and screens on which to mount them can be hired from CMS.

Footnotes

1. Themes and titles conceived by Joyce Henry (West Worthing Baptist Church). Used with permission.

5

Avoiding the ruts

Ideas for special world-mission events

'Next Sunday our speaker will be Ebenezer Giles-Smith who was a missionary in Timbuktu from 1937 to 1965. The service will be followed by a simple lunch after which Ebenezer and his wife, Agnes, will show vintage film footage of their pioneering work.'

As the secretary intones the notices there is a sudden flurry of rustling as everyone consults their diary to find a good reason for not coming next week. The mission mobiliser sighs. Why bother?

Most world-mission events centre around missionary speakers, although hopefully not like Ebenezer and Agnes! They are expected to come with exciting stories and preferably a video or slides.

Disadvantages of the traditional approach

The speaker/slideshow format takes little time and effort to arrange. All that is required of the hosting church is to listen politely and appear reasonably interested. The main input is left in the already full hands of the visiting missionary. However, such meetings rarely attract the non-supporters of mission whom you most want to come.

Relying wholly upon missionary speakers for your church's mission education has the additional drawback that it is not always easy to find suitable speakers available when you want them. Not all missionaries are gifted speakers, no matter how competent they are in their own practical field of service. Even the most charismatic of communicators may find it difficult to be dynamically enthusiastic when delivering their umpteenth talk to yet another gathering of impassive strangers.

Leaving the comfort zone

Organising interactive events using role-play exercises, discussion groups, culture-sampling activities or social evenings with a global theme is hard work. It is also risky. These types of events may not be well received by the older generation who form the majority of mission supporters.

We need to be prepared to take risks, however, if we want mission support to increase and candidates for mission to continue to be forthcoming. We must be prepared to present world-mission energetically, imaginatively and relevantly if we are to raise its profile effectively.

Advantages of the inter-active approach

Traditionally churches arrange just one annual world-mission event. This once-a-year thrust is less hassle to organise, especially for many mission mobilisers who do several jobs and have neither the time nor the energy for more than one major event a year. Holding a number of mission events throughout the year, however, enables some experimentation: practical projects, social events with a message, finance-raising efforts, *and* the occasional missionary speaker.

Having a number of events also enables you to focus in depth on several of the missionaries or areas in which the church is interested, rather than having to choose one and leave the rest for another year.

An all-age, activity-based approach makes mission education 'specials' accessible to everyone, enabling families to come along together and often drawing in fringe-members, unchurched relations and friends as well. These events can become welcome opportunities for people to enjoy fellowship as they relax and take part in different activities together. Mission 'specials' like this will be more memorable than the hymn—prayer format of an old-fashioned mission Sunday.

Decreasing the risk factor

Being sensitive to people's preferences is very important, but fear of how something different may be received should not inhibit you so much that you never dare to experiment and try something new. The risk involved in breaking new ground largely depends on the relationship you have established with the rest of the church. You can coax people to try all sorts of new ideas if they trust you and you have a good track-record.

Aiming to achieve a thoughtful balance between traditional and new methods helps to ensure that everyone is catered for, enabling you to recruit younger people without losing the support of faithful long-timers.

Try to involve as many people as possible in the planning of an event. This makes it their event and helps guarantee their presence on the day.

Assessing the practicalities

Responsibility for organising a special event can be shared among the members of the mission action-group or other organisations within the church.

Church premises with a number of side rooms are naturally suitable for multi-activity programmes, though a large hall can also be divided up into smaller sections to house separate concurrent activities. How about pausing for a moment and drawing a rough plan of your church's layout to help you think about the possibilities?

Events with a difference

Ideas can be gleaned from visiting other mission promotion events; reading missionary magazines and Christian newspapers; taking advantage of training sessions and area meetings where you can compare notes with other mission mobilisers; consulting with the church liaison officers of the societies with which you are linked.

Studying the methods which the secular world employs to educate and advertise in order to raise people's interest levels and win their custom can also be

---

Using your premises imaginatively

● One area could house an exhibition or be transformed into a representation of another country where people can taste samples of food, hear sounds, handle artefacts and see pictures of everyday life from that area. Think of the 'living displays' popular in museums and historic sites nowadays, or the world-mission experiences which you may have visited at Greenbelt, Spring Harvest and other Christian Festivals. Could you do something similar on a smaller scale?

● Use side rooms for showing a video, slides, or computer games downloaded from missionary societies' Web-sites.

● How about converting one area into a shop selling fairly traded foodstuffs and Third-World crafts, or books on world-mission?

● A larger room could be set out for more energetic activities such as team games with a missionary theme.

● Maybe you could allocate a room for donations of second-hand tools, type-writers, sewing machines or Christian books to send out to other countries.

● What about setting aside a room for children to do face-painting, make instruments, puppets or a banner, or take part in a drama workshop?

---

enlightening. Some of these may be adapted to raise the profile of world-mission in your church and attract new supporters.

You and your team will probably come up with all sorts of ideas once you get away from the speaker format, and can have great fun inventing your own activities. If a particular idea is well received, why not send it to mission headquarters for inclusion in their magazine or church resource packs?

A taste of France

When one mission mobiliser realised that her church's missionaries were due to visit the same weekend as Bastille day, she and her team organised a Revolution Day in the church grounds, drawing on French culture for ideas.

Finding out how it feels

One family fun-day I organised was to help people value the gift of sight. Our missionaries were involved with a programme to prevent river-blindness in Central Africa.

The event began with an entertaining exercise to show how much we rely on sight. We then separated into smaller groups for further activities to help us find out, messily at times, how difficult everyday life can be for the blind and visually impaired. Afterwards we met together again for a short final session about our missionaries' work.

A Latin Link experience

The comparative formality of the morning service on Latin Link Sunday at another church was followed by an authentic South American lunch, after which people were able to try different, less formal activities around the premises.

Party games

Popular party games can often be adapted for a mission theme.

- Paired words. Guests are given a word or phrase when they arrive and have to find their pair: for example 'snake bite' and 'antidote'; 'British' and 'Embassy' or words paired according to language.
- Picture challenge. Fix numbered pictures from missionary magazines to the walls. The task is to identify which parts of the world they depict.
- Treasure hunt. Everyone is given a list of questions about a specific country, the answers to which are written on postcards hidden around the premises. See how many they can match up within the time-limit.
- Word-game. Your missionaries could provide a selection of foreign words for use in 'Call my bluff' with teams attempting to pick the real meaning from a selection of true and false definitions.

The missionary guest

Whilst it is good to experiment with using a variety of ways to raise the profile of world-mission, there will always be room for hearing missionaries talk about their work, especially if they are gifted at public speaking.

Arranging a world-mission Sunday

Sundays can be opportunities in their own right or used to reinforce the mission theme introduced by an informal Saturday programme.

A Sunday service, hopefully not just attended by mission enthusiasts, provides a good opportunity to make the most of a missionary speaker. However, their input does not necessarily have to be a straight talk. Maybe an interview would be more appropriate. Consult them about what form they would prefer their input to take.

Arranging a speaker-centred event

Speakers appreciate being given detailed information, such as whether they are just to speak or are expected to lead the worship too; what worship patterns your church favours; the age range of their audience; whether it is possible to show slides or a video; if an overhead projector is available; how much time they have been allocated. These guidelines will help them be geared towards the needs and expectations of your church. It is all common sense really, if you think about what you would want to know if you were going somewhere new to give a talk.

Don't leave it all to the missionary!

You can make a world-mission Sunday service special in a number of additional ways. Why not add a world flavour to your worship by including one or two hymns and songs in other languages?

Church members from ethnic minorities could have some input into the service, to teach you something of their traditional style of worship.

Making sure people come

Even the best planned and most exciting of events will fail if inadequately publicised. Advertising your event well in advance is essential, making use of anyone you know who has the ability and resources to produce well-designed posters and fliers.

Mission events can be good opportunities for fellowship with people from other churches. Consider the possibility of advertising your event more widely and opening it to all the churches in your locality.

Involving as many people as possible in the actual running of the event not only ensures their own presence but also encourages them to invite other people since they have a vested interest in the event's success.

Mission events need no longer be the Cinderella of church life. Thanks to the many resources available, plus a generally greater flexibility about what is considered 'allowable', an exciting new range of possibilities is opening up for those prepared to rise to the challenge.

Resource materials

Liturgy and worship
- *A Still Place of Light* (USPG, 1990). Prayers from around the world.
- *Let all the world* (USPG, 1990). Worship material from around the world.
- David Peacock and Geoff Weaver (eds.), World Praise; Songs from around the world (Marshall Pickering, 1993).
- *Prayers Encircling the World* (SPCK, 1998). An international anthology of contemporary prayers.
- Maren C. Tirabassi and Kathy Qonson Eddy, *Gifts of many cultures:* (Cleveland, Ohio: United Church Press, 1995). Worship resources.

Resource and ideas packs
Check out missionary magazines for ideas sections and pull-out supplements.
- AIM: *Church Starter Pack and Youth Pack.*
- BMS: *Power Pack* Pages.
- CMS: *Takeaways.*
- Global Connections: *Global Action Resource Guide.*
- WBT: *Ideas Bank.*

Resource packs for specially designated weekends

Individual societies e.g. BMS, CMS and Tearfund advertise these. They usually focus on a different theme each year. Copies of packs produced for previous years may still be available.

6

Your money or . . .!

The vexed question of finance-raising

There is tremendous pressure on all of us to give money to a plethora of good causes, both Christian and secular. The sheer number of genuine and deserving organisations pleading for our help and support can result in 'compassion fatigue', with people simply switching off when yet another need is mentioned. Christians are affected too, so how does raising money for mission fit into your brief as mission mobiliser?

Is money-raising justifiable?

Some Christians are turned off by the term 'fund-raising'. For others it presents no problem.

Where do faith and God's provision fit in? Is it right to organise special efforts in order to raise money for Christian causes, or is it more biblical to keep quiet and leave this as a private matter between the individual and God? Huge differences of opinion exist concerning these issues and your answers will largely depend upon your particular spiritual base.

Sending agencies used to fall into two main categories: those who paid their missionaries a set salary out of central funds, and 'faith' missions, whose personnel relied on unsolicited gifts. There have, however, been changes in recent years concerning the whole issue of finance and fund-raising. Letting one's financial needs be known is no longer automatically interpreted as a lack of faith, although some societies still require their personnel 'simply' to pray for the money they need. This latter approach depends on Christians being sensitive to God's prompting and willing to respond. Human frailty means this ideal has not always been realised. So some sending organisations require prospective missionaries to raise promises of regular gifts from their supporters before leaving for their placement, thus ensuring a guaranteed income to cover basic living expenses.

Your role in finance-raising

Most of us find it hard to talk about money at church. Nevertheless, both missionary organisations and individual missionaries need financial backing in order to fulfil God's calling. An important part of your responsibility, therefore, is to remind people constantly of the monetary needs of world-mission and, where possible, to influence how your church organises its giving.

Encouraging your church to set an annual target is one way of giving them a goal and involving more people. Alternatively, an agreed fraction of the church's annual income could be designated for mission, including the financing of resources for your mission education programme. Both are preferable to relying on arbitrary appeals or the income from missionary boxes held by a few enthusiastic people.

Mission education stimulates giving

A well-resourced, imaginative mission education programme plays a vital part in money raising. The more people know, the more likely they are to decide that mission is important and be willing to support it financially.

The attitude of the leadership is vital too. If mission never features in their teaching programme, the responsibility to give has little hope of becoming part of people's thinking.

Even when people have become motivated to give, the battle is not necessarily over. Many people are distrustful of how charities allocate money, and quick to criticise what they see as wastefulness or inefficiency. 'I'll give if you can guarantee the money reaches the people it's intended for,' is a common attitude.

Your basic education programme could include making sure the annual financial statements of the societies your group supports are available, so people can see how 'their' money is being used.

How to release money for mission

Voluntary gifts

- Tax payers can increase the value of their gifts by using covenants or Gift Aid. These schemes enable a registered charity to reclaim tax already paid on the money given.
- People can be encouraged to include a bequest to a missionary organisation in their will.
- Mission boxes enable people with low incomes, such as children or the unemployed to set aside money for missions.
- Most people prefer to give to specific individuals or projects rather than to an impersonal central fund. Several societies organise annual target appeals for particular areas of need. These provide a useful focus for giving over a limited time-span.

Keeping people up to date

Regularly publicising different methods of giving and making up to date information leaflets freely available keeps up the challenge.

As in other aspects of support-raising, the cost of a few stamps, telephone calls or finding information via the Internet is well worth the benefit of keeping in touch with fresh ideas and options as they are produced.

Keeping people interested

Simple charts and pictures showing how much has been raised for a specific appeal help everyone to keep track of progress. Think of something relevant to the project or society you are supporting. SIM's *Missions Idea Notebook* suggests a sketch of a wall of blank bricks with each brick representing a set amount to be filled in as the money is raised. Alternatively a suitable map, photo or drawing could be cut up and the picture gradually re-assembled like a jigsaw as the money is given.

Making money-raising fun

Instead of just using the usual bag or plate, why not use Smartie tubes, decorated yoghurt pots, glass jars or small plastic tubs and bottles? Introducing an element of competition can be very effective, seeing how many pots each organisation in the church can fill, or who can cram the most coins into a small jar.

Collecting small change

People respond well when asked to give in small amounts – it feels manageable and yet soon adds up. Many people set aside their small change anyway, because coins of small value are fiddly to handle.

You could try 'The Great Penny Race': divide the group into two (having asked them to come prepared with 1p and 2p coins). Get each team to line up their coins across the floor. The longest line wins. The introduction of friendly rivalry and fun wins a much better response than the usual tradition of special envelopes for people to pick up and use.

Another idea is a special Advent Appeal, for which you need to make candle-shaped holders out of plastic bottles into which people place their small change week by week.[1] Disciplining ourselves to set aside money for others at the most pressured spending time of the year adds to the meaning of the advent season, as well as adding a significant amount to the yearly mission total.

Small coins can also be used to cover a map, poster or relevant picture displayed on a flat surface in the building where you meet for worship.

A little imagination can transform appeals from something which switches people off to something which switches them on. They may even begin to look forward to seeing what you will dream up next!

Other ideas

Those without a regular income could be encouraged to use abilities such as jam-making, knitting, baking, woodwork or painting, to raise money for mission. Or you could hold a 'promise auction', whereby people can sell their services as baby-sitters, car washers or gardeners to one another. In a silent auction, people donate items which are displayed around a room for viewing. Bidders write their name and bid on a piece of paper placed by each, and the highest bidder gets the goods.

Some Christian organisations auction donated goods in aid of missionary societies. Suitable items include jewellery, pictures, furniture, vases, clocks and collectibles. Missionary Auctions are held during the year, the proceeds of which go to the society of your choice. Legacy forms are also available for anyone wishing to leave their house and/or contents to be sold as a parting gift in aid of world-mission. (See the 'Further information' section at the end of this chapter.)

Stamps, pre-decimal and foreign coins, old badges especially military and other forces badges, postcards, cigarette and tea cards, and very old Christmas and birthday cards can be sent to specialist dealers who sell them in aid of mission. Surf the Internet or try the reference section of the public library for details.

The profit from ticket sales for special events can also be designated for missionary causes. Finally there is sponsorship, for which the possible variations-on-a-theme are limited only by the boundaries of human inventiveness and eccentricity.

'Stewardship can be interesting. A little imagination and a lot of enthusiasm lift it out of the ordinary and make it something very much alive. Even the youngest can understand and participate. Fund raising should be understood in its proper perspective. It is not just a means of squeezing a few more pennies out of people, it is providing frequent opportunities for people to give generously as good stewards.'[2]

The importance of prayer

It is prayer, however, which really makes a difference. Prayer is more important than methods and ideas, however original or clever. Pray that those whom you teach about mission and its needs will be moved by the Holy Spirit and their love for Jesus. Pray that the Father will prompt his people to be generous and sacrificial in their giving.

Further information

Collecting boxes, envelopes, and leaflets about giving are available from individual societies.

Information brochures from **Northwood Missionary Auctions**, and **Wallington Missionary Auctions** detailing what sort of valuables can be sold to raise money for missions. (See section VI of the Directory for addresses.

Footnotes

1 For further details, see Activity sheet A9, *Power Pack* (BMS).

2 *Missions Ideas Notebook*, p.38, (SIM, 1975).

7

Never too young . . .

Educating children and young people

My childhood memories of Mrs Rumbol are still vivid. Sitting on my little wooden chair one Sunday afternoon in the Sunday School, I looked and listened in awe. Mrs Rumbol actually existed! No longer a name at the end of a letter from somewhere far across the sea, she was here, in the flesh, alive and touchable – a real-life missionary. Not only that, she was *our* missionary. It was so exciting. Her letters continued to be read to us over the following years, and she became part of our lives, more real to us now because we had seen her for ourselves. That personal missionary link played its part in kindling my own lifelong interest in overseas mission, and I will always be grateful to our Sunday School leader.

The church's responsibility to educate children about world-mission

Mission education tends to be targeted at the upper teens and early twenties who are regarded as having a unique freedom from responsibilities, coupled with tremendous energy and a desire to do something practical to help – all of which can be very useful in terms of mission.

Mission education is given a low priority when it comes to pre-schoolers, children of primary school age groups and the lower teens. Yet we know that the influences brought to bear on a child in its early years mould what that child becomes and believes in later life. With this in mind, Fred Stainthorpe writes:

> Every teaching system should include an element of world-mission. In bringing young children to faith we should aim to mobilise their imagination, zeal and curiosity to gain a world knowledge of the church and a desire to serve in it. If we leave it until later their views may well narrow to their more immediate circle of interests. Whoever then tries to introduce world-mission to them could be asked, 'If it is so important now, why were you silent about it earlier?' As the twig is bent so the tree will grow. [1]

Why children are left out

'But what have children to offer?' you may ask. 'They have little and are limited in what they can understand and do.'

That is not God's opinion! The Bible clearly teaches God's fondness for using the weak and humble, those traditionally discounted by the world and, unfortunately, all too often by the church.

Exposing children to the thrill of being part of what God is doing across the world can have unnerving repercussions in the church as a whole. Are you prepared for this? Children, like missionaries, have the potential to make life uncomfortable for us. They remind us of what we should be doing but are often afraid to. They challenge our apathy, lack of faith, and introspection, and we do not necessarily welcome this.

Some reasons why we fail to cater for children in our missionary programmes are:

● We are short-sighted.
● Our image of mission is out-of-date.
● We do not really believe in their ability to be involved.
● We don't know how! [2]

At one time we might have been able to blame a lack of suitable materials and ideas, but this shortfall is now being addressed, though sadly the subject of missions is still not automatically an integral part of published Sunday School teaching-programmes. An increasing number of good resources are now being made available. It is time we remembered that the gospel which we teach our children is no different from the one for adults. Jesus calls us to be his disciples, whatever our age, so that, together, we may share him with everyone, everywhere.

Why children should not be left out

A number of missionaries testify to having first heard God's call to serve him overseas while they were still children. Is *your* church giving its children the opportunity to hear that call, as well as to be involved right now in his work worldwide? We have no right to expect young people in their late teens and early twenties to develop a sudden interest in missions or volunteer for missionary service, if they have not been actively encouraged to do so during the previous decade of church attendance.

Assessing your own church

Consider the following questions:

How much, and how imaginatively, is overseas mission included in the teaching programmes and activities run for under 15s in your church?

What happens to them during mission events? Do you run a separate programme for them or one which includes them?

Is mission included in your Sunday School, Junior church, children's club, mother and toddler group, play-group, all-age worship, holiday club?

Starting off

As in every area of planning a mission education programme, it is important to consult with those in leadership. It makes life easier if those working with the younger age groups can be persuaded that mission matters, especially since it is the adults who finance the church and plan its programme and priorities.

Sending agencies are investing an increasing amount of time and energy in the production of videos, drama scripts, games, books, activity packs and special fund-raising projects for children.

Games and quizzes, too, can now be downloaded from various missionary Web-sites and it probably won't be long before virtual reality computer games become an everyday part of the mission education resources scene.

If you spend some time initially contacting different societies to find out what is currently available, you will have the information and samples ready to whet the appetites of those who are responsible for running the children's and young people's work, as soon as they begin to show an interest. Then you will be able to sort out with them what would be most appropriate to use in your church situation. Some examples of resources currently available are given at the end of this chapter.

Making sure materials are used

Once you have the backing of your church and a good basic stock of suitable materials, there is still some work to be done if you are to ensure the resources are actually used. One way might be to invite the children's leaders to work with you in planning an all-age mission event.

If there is good co-operation between your group and others in your area, you could suggest sharing the acquisition of resources. This will increase your range of materials significantly whilst decreasing the amount of money spent. (Due to production costs, not many quality materials for children are free-of-charge.) In addition to church use, there might be opportunities to use your materials in local schools or children's clubs, thus getting extra value for money out of your initial investment.

Children need to be *doing*

Teaching children about overseas mission, and helping them to grow into world citizens, is not something to be limited to Sundays. Church-based toddler groups, playschools, holiday clubs and midweek activities all spell opportunities to include global issues and introduce youngsters to an awareness of other environments and cultures.

Role-play, drama and imagination teach far more than flannelgraphs and colouring sheets. Learning through play in this way can be very messy and time consuming, but it is great fun and very effective. Such experiences can create a lasting impression on young lives.

Noisy activities can be supplemented with readings from missionary story-books or by showing one of the many mission videos produced for children. Make use of all the resources that have been prepared: videos, books, leaflets, flannelgraphs, slidesets, ideas sheets, colouring books, children's clubs, resource packs, computer games. These are valuable in their own right but tend to have even more impact when used with an activity about a particular aspect of living in another country, or a specific theme. Children like the chance to experience things for themselves, rather than just hearing about them.

Play activities with mission themes

- Help the children discover the unfair distribution of wealth in the world by preparing a table of food, with a small selection of nice foods, (biscuits, mini-chocolate bars, small bowls of crisps), and plenty of plain food (dry bread, or scoops of plain rice or mashed potato). Let each child pick a numbered paper strip from the leader's hand, making sure the number is hidden from view. Then get them to queue up in number order. The first few get a good choice, while later ones have little choice and unappetising fare. The inevitable cries of 'It's not fair!' will open up opportunities to discuss alternatives such as sharing the good things with those who didn't get a chance to have them.

- Small children can get a taste of the desert by walking barefoot across a tray of sand. It feels nice until a few small stones and other bits are added (nothing sharp or dangerous of course), and then it is not much fun.[3]

- The plight of the homeless can be simulated by providing old boxes and sheets of cardboard for the children to build shelters, preferably out of doors. They are fun to hide in, but what happens when a hose is turned on to simulate rain? How does it feel to squat inside a soggy, smelly mess?[4]

- If a small patch of bare earth is accessible for a midweek club or activity day (maybe the church grounds or someone's garden), ask the children to see how deep a hole they can dig with simple tools? It will be hard work, especially if it hasn't rained recently. How long would it take to dig a well?

- What is it like having to walk for days to get to a doctor? Build a simple assault course for the children to go round in pairs, carrying a large doll or teddy on a stretcher between them. A sturdy table becomes a mountain, a series of stools with buckets of water in between forms a swamp, and garden netting fastened to the floor simulates thick undergrowth. Take it in turns to see who can carry their patients over the hostile terrain to the clinic and deliver them intact and in the quickest time.[5]

● In some countries, people have to walk for miles to collect water. Water is heavy! Provide a large container of water at one end of the church car park or garden. Line the children up at the other end in teams, and provide each with a small basin or bucket and a small plastic pot. Each child takes it in turn to walk to the container, fill their pot with water and carry it back. How many trips does it take to fill their team's bucket? How heavy is the bucket when full? Who is strong enough to pick it up? How far can they carry it? Think of a place the children know which is six miles away, to give them an idea of distance. Ask them to imagine walking there carrying the full bucket of water, then say a brief prayer thanking God for taps!

● A puppet can be a useful messenger for delivering up to date world-mission news. It is often easier to be uninhibited if hiding behind the persona of a puppet, and children will listen far more readily to a dramatic presentation like this than to a straight talk.

Opportunities for social action

Another way to exploit youngsters' energy and need to *do* something is by suggesting one of the schemes which offer them the opportunity to be involved in a practical way.

● The organisation Love Russia will send a free CD of the musical *The Old Russian Shoemaker* to any church or school seriously considering a performance to raise money for the organisation. The CD is so designed that a cast can either mime the whole musical or mime the story and sing accompanied by the backing tracks. The money raised goes mainly to work among orphanages in Russia and other projects, including a hospital in Moscow and a training establishment for teenagers leaving the orphanages.

● Samaritan's Purse is a Christian charity that runs an appeal at Christmas asking groups or families to fill a shoebox with gifts suitable for a child, including a signed Christmas card and a donation to cover transport – it costs just over £1 to deliver each box.

● Oasis Trust run periodically updated special schemes for youngsters wanting to use their energy and imagination to help others. They also offer short-term opportunities overseas.

These are just a few examples of what can be done to get young people looking to the world beyond their own immediate environment, to foster their concern for the needs of others, and to generate a wider perspective on life.

Mission education in the home

As the adults in the church catch the vision, parents can be encouraged to include overseas mission in their family life.

Sandra Kimber has several suggestions for ways to do this:

● Offer hospitality to people from overseas, such as international students or visiting missionaries.

● Use *You can Change the World* or missionary story books at bedtime.

● Write as a family to another family overseas.

● Go on a short-term project as a family, with YWAM's King's Kids. (Christian Vocations' *Short-term Service Directory* includes details of one or two other organisations which also accept families who want to get involved with helping overseas.)

Children learn so much about priorities and values from their early years at home. Talking about other countries and cultures, problems in the world, individual missionaries or people groups, can become a natural part of family life. Parents can watch children's news bulletins on TV with them; have maps and pictures available or on display somewhere in the house; make a collage or frieze with their child to decorate a bedroom wall; involve the children in choosing a missionary calendar with colour pictures for keeping track of engagements. (My mother used to hang the missionary calendar on the door of the smallest room. The location guaranteed it was looked at several times every day!)

Have fun as a family by testing your flying skills with MAF's *Lifeline* computer game, available on CD-ROM from Sunrise Software (see section II of the Directory).

Families could consider adopting a country or a child as a focus for their prayers and practical support. Plenty of agencies advertise child-sponsorship programmes.

Involving children in finance-raising

Children like to be practical in their caring, which is why they often end up fund-raising. Collections of drinks cans, newspapers, foil, stamps, and so on, represent money when passed on to recycling organisations. Even little children can participate in this, with adult help in co-ordinating their efforts. Alternatively, children can be encouraged to give small coins, perhaps going without a favourite treat one week and bringing the money to place on a picture or chart at their Sunday or mid-week group.

Children are very aware of the world and its needs, thanks to television. We fail God and the multitudes of people still to be reached with the gospel if we deny children the opportunities to be involved, and if we fail to recognise and encourage their motivation and enthusiasm during their early years.

Teaching methods geared for today's generation

One way to get young people involved is by showing them they have something valuable to contribute. Stuart Blythe writes: 'The encouragement given to young people to be mission motivated and involved, remains in many places not simply out of date in terms of presentation, but worse, patronising and shallow in terms of content.'[6]

Because of this ineffective approach, there is what Phil Marsden refers to as 'a massive untapped resource in many of our churches today – young people.' He writes, 'These young activists are ready to take on the world – to fight for freedom, challenge injustice, stand up for the poor and oppressed. They want to make a difference.'[7]

Has your mission action-group ever invited young people to join them, to represent their peers' views and ideas, and help to plan the mission programme and special events? (This will only work if the action-group really is prepared to listen to them.)

Energy, enthusiasm and imagination are all necessary in maintaining a global vision in our young people. The largely paper-based teaching methods of yesterday no longer work. Mission education is being developed to appeal to the adolescent audiences of today through computer-generated information on a large video screen or video wall, drama, modern songs, a live telephone or video link with a missionary, games and role-playing exercises designed to give insights into other cultures, interactive walk-through displays at festivals such as Greenbelt, roadshows touring nation-wide, Web-sites which can be visited while surfing the Internet.

Drama scripts, games and details of projects specifically geared towards young people can be obtained from the sending agencies, who are constantly trying to keep pace with the changing lifestyles and communication styles preferred by the teens and twenties. Resources cannot remain static if they are to be meaningful and attractive for this age group, so it is best to contact the agencies to see what is currently on offer.

Other ideas for teenagers

Holidays

A few organisations, notably WEC, organise annual summer camps. Youngsters who go to these enthuse about them, catch a glimpse of the wider world, and go back for more. Sadly, however, not so many of these holidays are available nowadays, but those which are come with a 'highly recommended' label.

Short-term experience

The biggest growth area in terms of cultivating the interest of young people focuses on the eighteen-plus age group. Short-term experience overseas, ranging from two weeks to two years, involves them in anything from street theatre to very practical maintenance work. This subject is explored further in the next chapter, but it is worth noting that some schemes are open to younger ages, or to families including children. Details can be found in the *Short-term Service Directory,* published annually by Christian Vocations. Children tend to be clearer and less inhibited about their faith than adults, but their zeal can often be dampened by a refusal to include them in evangelism, and they are lost before they are finally considered to be 'grown-up enough'.

Prayer is vital

Above all else, pray that God will inspire you, along with the youth workers, as you seek to encourage children and young people to become mission-supporters and missionaries not just in the future, but *now.*

Summary of resources

Books
- Jill Johnstone, *You can Change the World,* (WEC, 1992)
- Daphne Spraggett, *You too can Change the World,* (WEC, 1996)
- Wycliffe Bible Translators have a small range of colouring / quiz books and story books for 4-10 year olds.
- See societies' own listings for a wide range of suitable literature including story books.

Clubs (with regular mailings)
- *Activist* (Tearfund). For 14+ age group.
- *Gobstopper Gardens* (Tearfund). For 7-10 year olds.
- *Stopwatch,* (Chime Worldwide). A special programme for children which includes an award scheme.
- *Umoja* (Tearfund). For 11-13 year olds.
- *WOW* (Windows on the World) club for children, (BMS).
- *WYnet team* (Wycliffe Bible Translators). For 13-18 year olds.

Computer Games
Lifeline (on CD-ROM). Available from MAF or Sunrise Software.
Explore societies' Web-sites for games to download.

Directories
- *Who? What? Where?* (Mission Computers). Listings of Christian resources for children and young people
- *Help!* (Chime Worldwide). Listings of over 300 resources for children.

Holidays
Summer camps: Extension Ministries, WEC. (An audio-visual presentation is available.)

Opportunities abroad:
- King's Kids, YWAM: Highfield Oval, Harpenden, Herts. AL5 4BX
- *Short-term Service Directory* (Christian Vocations: published annually).

- Youth Departments: various missionary organisations.

Packs
- *Decision-making games for teenagers* (AIM International).
- *Prayer Ideas Pack* (AIM International). A resource pack for children / youth workers, with simple but imaginative ideas for helping children to pray for overseas mission.
- *Supercez Action Pack* (MAF). Activities for the under-12s.
- Various books, information and activity packs can be ordered from CAFOD, CMS, SIM (UK) and WEC.
- OMF have produced slide-sets for children.
- *World-mission Resources Pack* (Echoes of Service). A loose leaf binder comprised of several units, with information and outlines for mission education amongst young people.

Practical projects
- Oasis Trust: projects such as *Big Take*.
- *Operation Christmas Child* (Samaritan's Purse). 'Fill a shoebox' Christmas appeal.
- *The Old Russian Shoemaker* (Love Russia). A musical production.
- Child support schemes: contact individual agencies such as Tearfund, Worldshare, Adopt-a Child and Child Rescue International.

Footnotes

1. Fred Stainthorpe, 'Open Line: World Mission Focus', (Baptist Times, 24th November, 1994).

2. Taken with permission from notes by Sandra Kimber entitled 'Giving Children a World Vision', (Chime Worldwide, 1966).

3. Ideas conceived by Cath Dunlop and used by permission of Chime Worldwide.

4. *Ibid.*

5. Adapted from *Power Pack*, Activity sheet A1, (BMS).

6. Stuart Blythe; 'Young People and Mission', (BMS *Missionary Herald*, July/August 1996).

7. Phil Marsden; 'Let Them get a Piece of the Action', (BMS *Missionary Herald*, July/August 1996).

8

'It could be you!'

Cross-cultural opportunities for everyone

Evangelism is a scary word for most Christians. John was no exception. He was one of the shyest boys I ever taught in Sunday School, so it was no surprise that he found the idea of 'proclaiming the gospel' in public pretty terrifying. He realised, however, that there were other ways to offer help to people less fortunate than himself, in the name of Christ. He also wanted to see the world so he enquired about opportunities for short-term service overseas, and eventually ended up spending the summer in Kenya with a team of Christians building a huge water storage tank for the local people. Later John returned to Kenya, with a different organisation, to teach for a year in a rural school.

For many people, going to other countries is an invaluable experience which often inspires long-term interest in mission. But those who cannot explore this option need not be excluded from the exciting first-hand experience of other cultures, for the world also comes to us.

A global village

People-groups once separated by awesome distances are increasingly being brought together by modern transport and transglobal communications systems. Familiarity and accessibility have shrunk the world into a global village.

Implications for world-mission

World-mission has changed too. It is no longer the one-way system of yester-year. We have increasing opportunities to welcome people from other cultures into our churches and our homes, as well as send workers out to them. We need the grace and humility to admit that we have often failed in mission within our own culture, and be prepared to listen to Christians from other countries who can teach and encourage us in our efforts to reach out to our neighbours.

Churches can develop direct links with congregations in other cultures, and exchange visits. Much mutual benefit can be gained from such two-way traffic, for world-mission and home mission are inextricably entwined. The one fuels the other.

Jerusalem – reaching those on our doorstep

In our multi-cultural society, ethnic groups rub shoulders everywhere. Few people will have to travel far to meet somebody from another cultural back-ground. Newsagent, doctor, nurse, teacher, lecturer, accountant, market-stall holder or waiter; sometime, somewhere, you will probably find yourself in con-tact with someone from a different ethnic background. How do you and your church regard these people? Do you ever try to get to know them, invite them into your home, your church, or share your leisure activities as friends? Do you sit with them at church, or at the parents' evening, or are you frightened off by an unfamiliar accent?

'Culture is something everyone else has!'

What does 'culture' mean? Roger Bowen defines it as 'the patterned way in which people do things together'.[1] He sees it both as a bridge which links one generation to another, and a wall which separates one group of people from another. 'Culture involves the beliefs, values, customs and institutions which bind a society together with a sense of identity, value, security and continuity . . . People cannot escape their own culture because it is within them; but they can defend themselves against another culture, or they can deliberately enter a new culture as the Son of God did when He was born as the man Jesus.'[2]

Part of the task of helping your church to become world Christians is to make them aware of the opportunities for first-hand encounters with other cultures. You can then show them how to make use of these.

Stepping outside the comfort zone

Are you reluctant to take a stand when neighbours constantly complain about the Asians living in your street? Stepping outside the safe parameters of our own culture can be a very frightening step, especially if the people we meet from other ethnic backgrounds are practising followers of another faith. Many Christians prefer to avoid the complex issues raised by talking with people from other faiths. Such dialogue can be both enlightening and enriching, yet often we do not even feel secure enough to dialogue with Christians from other denominations.

'We discover God when we lose ourselves in mission but we lose God when we try to stay secure in sheltered territory.'[3]

Helping people to cross the cultural barriers

Imagine you have persuaded some people in your church to look for cross-cultural opportunities on their own doorstep. What next? Initial training sessions or discussion groups for those interested will not only help them to compare notes and support one another, but will also guard against their making the sort of blunders which might bring their efforts to a halt after just one attempt.

What do they need to know?

Firstly, they need to recognise their own culture. Problems occur when we assume that something as basic as body language is universal. Eunice Okorocha cites the following as an example:

'. . . avoiding eye contact is a sign of respect in most African and Asian cultures but this can indicate insecurity in western cultures. For some cultures it is important to stand close to someone during a conversation and to touch when making a point or when the conversation becomes interesting, but elsewhere this is intimidating or uncomfortable.'[4]

Culture dictates the way we interact socially, moulding our expectations and understanding of people. It defines basic aspects of everyday life such as table manners or how we greet one another. It influences our world-view, our priorities and our attitudes, yet it is such an integral part of us that we are unaware of it until we meet a different culture and realise there are other ways of doing things.

Preparing together

A good starting-point is to organise an informal evening of discussion for those interested, starting off with a role-play exercise or drama sketch to highlight the possible misunderstandings which arise when people from two cultures meet. This can be conducted seriously, or presented as a comic 'how not to do it', (bearing in mind that funny sketches are more memorable than lectures).

This could then be followed by group work in which people try to identify and talk about different issues raised by the role-play or drama. The missionaries or sending organisations with whom you are linked may be able to send some ideas. (Some helpful resources are listed at the end of the chapter.)

Invite a specialist (not necessarily a Christian), to lead a session on how to be a friend to people from other ethnic backgrounds, including what pitfalls to avoid.

Read all about it . . .

One easy way to educate people about other cultures is to provide missionary biographies for them to read. Why not hold a missionary book day, when people lend each other a good read? Alternatively, ask people to donate their copies as stock for a small lending library. Information about other cultures and problems which can occur is a natural part of such accounts. Books written primarily for prospective missionaries, such as Tearfund's *Prepared to Serve,* have helpful chapters about other cultures and faiths.

Giving hospitality or help

Some may want to open their home to an acquaintance from a different ethnic background with whom they already have a natural point of contact, perhaps through work, a shared interest or waiting for children together at the school gates.

Others might offer hospitality to an overseas student. International Student Christian Services have workers available to advise and help any individuals or churches who want to offer friendship in this way. Overseas students may feel especially lonely during weekends and long vacations when, unlike fellow students, they cannot just pop home to see friends and family. Genuine friendship and practical care speak volumes and may well inspire the question 'Why?' which then opens a door for words to back up the actions.

Judaea — looking further afield

Once your church has begun to extend the hand of friendship to those beyond their own culture, it is time to consider cross-cultural contact farther afield. Recently, many churches have formed partnerships with churches in other countries.

Some links were made initially when churches organised convoys of aid to specific areas of need. This became particularly fashionable when Eastern Europe started to open up, and some long-lasting partnerships have resulted. Such opportunities are not limited to Europe. One church in north-east England has forged a lasting friendship with a church in Africa, with representatives from each visiting the other.

Windows of opportunity

Spasmodic hit-and-run forays into other countries are not overly helpful. A long-term commitment to one small congregation is of more lasting value. It can be costly to sustain such a commitment, and there is always the danger that an unexpected political crisis may sabotage months, even years of effort, and make communication impossible at any time. This can be heartbreaking, but personal and emotional involvement helps a church to empathise with Christians overseas, developing a better understanding of what they face.

Make the most of windows of opportunity for sharing directly in the life of congregations overseas. Mutual encouragement is a wonderful way to experience what it means to be part of the world church.

Something for everyone

A cross-cultural, church-based partnership can be organised in such a way that everyone is encouraged to feel they have a part to play. Direct personal contact makes all the difference. Opportunities to collect and deliver specifically requested items, or to get involved in practical projects such as repairing buildings or providing equipment, literature or medicine, receive a much better response than some vague appeal. People can take it in turns to make up the

Reaching ethnic minorities at home:

Training and action

- A series of short practical training courses including cross-cultural evangelism and reaching people of other faiths is being developed by The Missionary Training Service.
- Cultural awareness workshops: Dr Eunice Okorocha: E-mail: Eokorocha@aol.com
- Hospitality for overseas students: International Student Christian Services.
- Correspondence courses, books and leaflets on Islam. Available in English and Urdu (Word of Life).
- TEFL courses: International Training Network (see Section II of the Directory).
- Web-evangelism (SOON): http://www.brigada.org/today/articles/web-evangelism.html Also
- Web-writing & webmaster resources: http://www.webauthors.org/guide/web-evangelism.html Includes free monthly newsletter.
- *Which World? Which God?* (Crosslinks). Video which explores ways in which we are all affected by the different cultures around us.

Further reading

Anne Cooper: *Heart to Heart: Talking with Muslim friends* (Word of Life, 1997).

Anne Cooper (ed.) *Ishmael my Brother* (Marc, 1993).

Evangelising Hindus and Buddhists (The Missionary Training Service, 1998).

Evangelising Muslims (The Missionary Training Service, 1998).

Guidelines for making contact with Asians in Britain (MAB: Interserve).

How to Make Disciples in Other Cultures (The Missionary Training Service, 1998).

Bill Musk *The Unseen Face of Islam: Sharing the Gospel with Ordinary Muslims* (Marc 1989).

Glenn Myers *The Arab World* (OM Publishing, 1998).

Sally Sutcliffe *Aisha my sister* (Solway, 1997).

Margaret Wardell and Ram Gidoomal *Chapatis for Tea. Reaching Your Hindu Neighbour: A Practical Guide* (Highland, 1994).

World Religions Overview (ISCS).

ISCS have produced information leaflets about: Animism, Buddhism, Hinduism, Islam, Judaism, Marxism, Secularism and Shintoism. (Available separately or as a set.)

teams who visit the partner-church. Return visits give everyone a chance to meet members of the other church. One South London church found their link with Albania was a good way of getting everyone involved. Those who could not go, prayed. Many contributed towards the cost of travel, and gave gifts to be taken out. As the visitors got involved in various aspects of church life alongside their Albanian brothers and sisters, they discovered new things about themselves and God, including new gifts to develop when they returned home which enriched the life of their own church.

Adopt a people

If a cross-cultural link is beyond your resources, why not adopt a people group through your missionaries or through societies such as Wycliffe Bible Translators or WEC? Getting to know one particular culture intimately can inject new life into your praying and general level of interest. There may be opportunities to take a team on a short visit to meet and possibly help individuals from the people group. Remember to liaise closely with those working long-term in the situation, following their advice about doing things in culturally acceptable ways.

Linking with a church or people group from another part of the world

Direct support for national Christians
● WorldShare.
● Amen.

Eastern Europe
● Radstock Ministries.

People Groups
● Vision 20, Wycliffe Bible Translators. (Includes cross-cultural training for anyone involved in actually going out to visit 'their' people group.)

Further reading
● *Accountability without control in cross-cultural Christian Partnerships* (WorldShare, 1994).
● *Unreached Peoples of the World* (The Missionary Training Service, rev. edn. 1999).

Samaria – even farther afield

How do people from your church view their holiday? Many will travel abroad but stay with their compatriots, eat their own national food, expect to communicate in English, and not seem bothered about making any real contact with the local inhabitants. What a missed opportunity!

'The tourist who stays safely by the hotel pool will have the same horizon he had at home . . . it is possible to travel half the way round the world as a tourist to visit new places, and yet never "be there" at all!'[5]

At the very least, visiting another country on holiday offers an opportunity to pray for that country while you are there. Have you ever thought about encouraging people to read about their holiday venue in *Operation World* and then to pray for its people while they are there?

Holidays with a difference

A small group could arrange a holiday together and prayer-walk the areas they visit. This needs to be done discreetly in countries open to tourists but closed to overt evangelistic activity. In some countries, however, you may be able to distribute Christian literature or encourage nationals by sharing fellowship with them even if you do not understand their language.

Collect brochures about Christian holidays to display in your church for a month after Christmas when most people are planning their holidays, or in early summer just before they zoom off for the summer break. Catch people's attention with a snappy title for your display and link it in with your service slot or magazine column.

In one Oak Hall brochure, someone recently returned from holiday comments: 'I feel that the trip was extremely worthwhile. It enabled me to learn and understand more about mission and I found the whole experience to be challenging . . .'

Tell a tourist

London is a great tourist spot but have you ever stopped to wonder how many countries are represented by these visitors? They come from every corner of the globe. As many as 104 nationalities have been recorded.[6]

How many of us view this as an opportunity to make personal contact with another culture for Christ?

Making the most of opportunities

Holiday-makers from other countries
- Tell a Tourist: London City Mission (Youth Department).

Holidays with a difference
- Oak Hall Holidays (tel. 01732 763131 for brochure or visit the Oak Hall Web-Site. http://www.oakhall.clara.net)
- WEC Extension Ministries.

. . . to the ends of the earth

'Lord, here I am, send me.' This is the ultimate response every mission mobiliser prays for and works towards. The list of vacancies, short or long term, is invariably longer than the list of volunteers.

For a limited period

Short-term opportunities for service overseas have mushroomed in recent years. Almost every major missionary society and relief organisation operates at least one scheme enabling people to offer their expertise, whether practical, educational, managerial or theological. Placements can be arranged for a period of weeks, months, a gap year or longer.

Short-term workers can provide a useful task force for helping with immediate specific needs. Although many schemes are geared towards younger people, an increasing number are run for middle-aged or retired folk. 'People in their 70s have been on short-term service – and gone back for more!'[7] There are even schemes for families.

It is a marvellous opportunity for those who may be unable to commit themselves for a long period to get involved in God's Kingdom worldwide. The variety of schemes and types of work are too many to list here, but you can obtain information from individual organisations or from one of the short-term service directories. Keep some of these on display for people to browse through.

Short-term placements are for people prepared to work hard as part of a team, giving up their rights and doing whatever is asked of them – all at their own expense. They are not designed for people looking for a temporary escape from pressure, or a chance to drop out till they get their life sorted. Short-term projects provide a life-changing way of finding out first-hand what living and working abroad are really like. Some volunteers go on to commit themselves to long-term service. Others become energetic advocates for mission.

One short-termer writes: 'I have been able to see mission life as it really is – not as I think it is. Living in another country also highlights the impact culture has on one's thinking and behaviour. I hope I have acquired a more global perspective.'[8]

As volunteers are usually required to raise a set amount of money, the whole church family can be involved. While abroad they need the same support as full-time missionaries. When they return, it is important to give them plenty of opportunities to share their experiences. The first-hand knowledge they have acquired will play a valuable part in increasing the church's awareness and interest in the world church. Cash in on this! No-one will want to miss hearing of their experiences.

Tentmakers – Christians in secular work abroad

Some people may have jobs that involve regular visits abroad. Some are even based in another country. Such employment offers a unique opportunity to exercise a Christian presence in an area where secular workers receive a warm welcome but missionaries do not. Some people might want to consider this when choosing or changing their career. However, it must be stressed that this is not an easy option.

Tentmakers, as Christians who take secular employment overseas are frequently called (after the apostle Paul who used his skill as a tentmaker to pay his way), can feel very much on their own. They may not receive the recognition which a career missionary might expect from both church-base and sending agency, since we are sometimes too narrow in our definition of 'real' missionaries. You can help Christians working regularly or permanently overseas to see the spiritual opportunities their position affords. You can also encourage your church to extend its understanding of the word 'missionary' by including them in its overall mission support programme of care and prayer.

Teaching English as a Foreign Language – TEFL

Teachers of English, both at home and abroad, are especially in demand now that English has become the accepted international language for many areas of modern life. Although it may prove difficult for those in business or industry to make meaningful contact with nationals, teaching English offers unique opportunities for person-to-person encounters. For a start, it brings the teacher into daily contact with the students, either in the classroom or the home.

More importantly, however, 'because students often want to learn about culture, beliefs and lifestyles as well as language, the teacher is able to share something of his or her own values. Discussion often continues outside the classroom, which can lead to deeper and closer relationships. This building of both professional relationships and personal friendships over a period of time encourages opportunities to share the Gospel in a natural and culturally sensitive way.'[9]

Training is available for those who want to try this particular option.

Reaching the world from your home

Almost anyone can make a practical contribution towards world-mission by typing labels, posting broadsheets such as Bientot and UPESI or marking Bible study courses for SOON (who send newspaper-style broadsheets and basic Bible courses all over the world).

Wycliffe Associates (UK) enables people based at home to use their time and abilities to support overseas workers in a variety of ways. These range from the very simple (for example posting prayer letters), to the more skilful (such as translating documents or conducting library research). Internet has opened up new opportunities for Christians to share the gospel worldwide without leaving home or native land. Writers and computer enthusiasts can be encouraged to explore this possibility. SOON Ministries has produced a comprehensive guide which can be downloaded from their Web-site.

People involved in these ways will also need the prayer support and interest of your church.

Something for everyone

Everyone can be a cross cultural missionary in one way or another nowadays. A multitude of ways of bringing church and world together is opening up for the next generation of mission mobilisers.

Footnotes

1. . . . *So I Send You*, p.82. Quoted with permission.

2. *Ibid.*

3. *Ibid.*, p.216.

4. Eunice Okorocha, 'Cultural clues to student guidance' (*The Times Higher Educational Supplement*, June 7th 1996). Quoted by permission of the author.

5. Barbara and Tom Butler, Just Mission, pp.9-10. Quoted with permission.

6. Short-term Service Directory, (Christian Vocations, 1966), p.54. Quoted with permission.

7. *Ibid.*, p.3.

8. *Ibid.*, p.57.

9. 'Class Act' edited by Phil Seager, (*Idea*, Jan/Feb/Mar 1998). Quoted with permission.

Short-term opportunities abroad.

Christian Directories
- *World Service Enquiry* (Christians Abroad)
- *Jobs Abroad Directory, Short-term Service Directory* and *Training Directory* (Christian Vocations).

Secular Directories

(Copies of these will probably be available in the reference section of your local library. They are also available from bookshops on the Internet.)
- *International Directory of Voluntary Work* (Vacation Work Publications, 1997).
- *Voluntary Agencies Directory* (NVCO Publications, 1999.)
- *Volunteer Work* (Central Bureau for Educational Visits and Exchanges, 1995).

Opportunities for getting involved at home

Bientot, SOON and UPESI. (See section IV of the Directory.)

Wycliffe Associates (See section IV of the Directory.)

Reading and training for tentmakers
- *The Challenge of Tentmaking* (Global Connections, 1999)
- *Tentmaking Missionaries* (The Missionary Training Service, rev. edn. 1999).

TASK offers a personal service of advice and training for professional, trades, and business people going overseas with a call to be involved in mission (see section II of the Directory.)

TEFL courses
- International Training Network (see section II of the Directory.)

9

What about the Third-World?

Sounding the trumpet for the exploited and underprivileged

The statistics are overwhelming.

'Between 15 and 30 million children spend their days surviving in the urban landscape of major cities, without access to the education and material resources that many other children take as the norm.'[1]

'Developing countries spend £83 billion a year on arms.'[2]

'Roughly every fifteen minutes a human being is blown up by one of the millions of anti-personnel landmines scattered indiscriminately around the world. Indeed even this is a conservative estimate, for many of the victims never make it to hospital. They are caught in remote places and die unaided and alone . . .'[3]

'Poor countries earn many times more through trade than they receive in aid, giving them the opportunity to reduce poverty and fund development. Too often, however, the injustices of international trade mean these remain missed opportunities.'[4]

Each year the amount which developing countries pay the West in debt repayments is about three times more than they receive in aid. These statistics are appalling but what is even more disturbing is our growing immunity to them. As Christians, however, we must not ignore them, neither can we afford to let them overwhelm us so much that we are incapable of any response. Bringing the world to your church includes exposing them to such facts. This is not in order to weigh them down with guilt but so that you can stir them into action by helping them see what they can do to make a difference.

Mission – preaching by words and actions

There is nothing new about seeing world-mission as something which includes the social and physical needs of the people to whom the gospel is brought. It was missionaries who first opposed the slave trade, and built schools and hospitals in many parts of the world.

They did not see their ministry as an 'either/or'. They regarded both physical and spiritual help as equally essential aspects of their work.

During the twentieth century, improvements in global communication resulted in more and more information about other parts of the world reaching the affluent societies of the North. Awareness increased with the availability of television. Actually seeing refugees and victims of famine, war and natural disaster on the news had more direct impact than simply hearing or reading the reports. The Christian relief agencies which were formed as a result have an important role to play. They remind us of our responsibilities with regard to worldwide physical human needs as well as preaching and teaching matters of faith, and enable us to act.

Today's society frowns on 'intolerant' Christians who say Jesus is the only means of salvation, and have the 'arrogance' to proselytise. Sadly, this unbiblical thinking has crept into the church, dampening our missionary zeal. As a result it may be harder to drum up support for evangelistic activity or Bible translation than for more politically correct aid and development.

Working out how to include both aspects of world-mission in the support you offer is a vital part of formulating a holistic mission programme, uniquely tailored to your church and determined by your particular understandings, interests and priorities.

People tend to have strong views on the subject so be prepared for prolonged and possibly vehement discussion as you consider these questions:

- Is part of your mission programme to be devoted to supporting aid and relief in the developing countries and areas which are in the news because of famine, war or natural disaster?

- If so, how much?
- Will you do this through societies with which you are already linked, or through a specialist in relief and development programmes such as Tearfund, Christian Aid or World Vision ?

Educating why

Enabling your church members to understand the background of the crises in the poorer parts of the world is very important, if they are to help bring about fundamental change by addressing the causes of poverty as well as its effects. Maybe an energetic member of your mission action-group could take responsibility for relief and development issues in order to stimulate action as well as giving within your church. The major relief agencies have produced a whole range of explanatory booklets plus details of practical initiatives.

A separate notice board to display newspaper cuttings of trouble spots around the world with suggestions for prayer and action could be useful. Alternatively, you could focus on these issues on your main missions board every so often. The editor of your church magazine might welcome a regular column, highlighting situations of suffering and deprivation, and giving prayer and action points.

Perhaps you could arrange a special awareness campaign in your church using some of the ideas suggested in chapter 5. Catchy titles like 'It just isn't fair!' or 'What about the workers?' will help to catch people's attention.

Other ways of helping besides giving money

Speaking out

Freedom of speech, and the democratic process, are privileges which we can exploit on behalf of those who are denied them. Public opinion really can make a difference, as long as people are taught what to say, how to say it and to whom.

Many crises need not be ongoing. Much injustice continues because it remains unchallenged. How much evil prevails because of our silence? It is time to encourage Christians to speak out; to persuade the leaders and industries of the developed world that people really want changes of policy in favour of the interests of the Third-World; to convince them that we are prepared to sacrifice our own interests. Politicians need to be reassured that reform does not spell political suicide. They are unlikely to be willing to take the risk without a clear mandate from the electorate.

This message will get across only if people actually write to their MP about issues like human rights, religious freedom, the cancellation of international debt, land-mines and aid which is conditional on arms sales.

- *Write letters for change* (available from Christian Aid), provides relevant addresses and guidance in writing letters to MPs.
- Christian Aid produce printed, addressed postcards on specific issues. The sender only has to sign, add a stamp and post it. Contact Christian Aid (campaigns) for details.
- Find out if prepared petitions or suggested wording for home-produced petitions on specific current issues are available from the organisations you support. Make sure you are on their mailing list if you want to receive details.

Spending out: fair-trade

Supporting fair-trade helps alternative trading organisations to provide and campaign for a regular, fair income for Third-World producers.

It does not only involve taking orders for Third-World crafts at Christmas, though that is an excellent thing to do. Fairly traded goods, including basic foodstuffs, are available all year round at some supermarkets. Putting pressure on them to supply more is one way of increasing the availability of fair-trade products. Imagine the impact if everyone in your church or group of churches wrote to the local supermarket asking them for more fairly traded goods and was prepared to back this up by buying the goods. Unfortunately many Christians are reluctant to change the shopping habits of a lifetime.

Another way to encourage people to buy Third-World products is to sell them on a regular basis at church. If this is open to the general public, maybe at a coffee morning, it can also strengthen links with the local community.

Your church could decide to use only fair-trade tea and coffee for in-house catering.

What about the whole issue of boycotting businesses which do not pay their workers a decent wage, and to shun retailers who stock their goods and thereby condone such malpractice? There is plenty of material for lively discussion here. The World Development Movement can supply relevant details.

Once we are aware of what is going on, our shopping trips can be a complicated exercise!

Materials which can help you

Relief agencies produce videos, study packs, posters and information to assist you in publicising both the needs and things people can do to help. Prayer diaries are available for individual use. Tearfund, Cafod, World Vision and Christian Aid all have literature which you can order, (usually at cost), covering a range of issues from landmines to commercial exploitation of children. They also provide imaginative, themed resource materials for Christmas, Harvest, and their own society promotion weekends.

Simulation, role-playing and board games are available from Tearfund and Cafod. All sorts of resources for use with children and young people, including in schools, can be obtained from both these organisations and from World Vision.

Your young people's group might want to take part in Christian Outreach's sponsored Sleep Out or World Vision's annual 24 Hour Famine.

Christian Aid organises different campaigns to address a variety of issues, and can provide you with information and materials, or you could register with Tearfund's Global Action network, which seeks to 'enable Christians to campaign on development issues from a biblical basis.'

Crafts, clothing and food can be ordered from both Tearcraft and Traidcraft.

Details of all the above can be found in the relevant resource catalogues.

Opportunities to get involved first-hand

In addition to the short-term opportunities mentioned in the previous chapter, opportunities exist for churches or groups of churches working on their own initiative. In latter years, many churches have seized the opportunity to organise their own regular transportation of aid to needy Christians in Eastern Europe.

One account of such a journey expresses the value of this work:

> Petronella was gobsmacked when we turned up at her home in Batiz . . .
> Petronella is a spastic. She is 18 years old and she spends her life on her bed, looked after entirely by her mother and her family . . . she has a perfectly good brain and a useless, twisted, almost paralysed body . . .
> We had driven 1,507 miles from Weymouth in a little hatchback to deliver her various pieces of specialised equipment aimed at making life easier for her and her parents . . .

Petronella's story illustrates the way in which we feel we have been called to serve in our very small way in Romania, getting involved in something small and almost insignificant, helping in a situation where local provision is inadequate or non-existent, and realising afterwards that God's hand was in it all along and that out of it bigger things come.[5]

There may be other churches near you who are already doing this kind of work. You may be able to join in with them. Alternatively you could approach one of the many societies involved in this area.

How to get involved

The following organisations would greatly value your help:
- Aid to Russian Christians, and Radstock: both seek to promote contacts between Christians from East and West.
- Partnership for Growth (formerly Link Romania) is an organisation through which people with practical skills can help with short-term projects. Drivers holding an HGV licence could give a few days to help with transportation of humanitarian aid.
- Love Russia accepts gifts of good quality clothing, shoes, musical instruments and toys. (Contact their office to arrange delivery.)

Your church might want to make a friendship link with a church, group, community or family, in Europe or a Third-World country, whom you could help and encourage in very specific ways. Alternatively you could consider focusing your interest and support on a specific project. A comprehensive list of specialist agencies can be found in the *UK Christian Handbook.*

To summarise

A Tearfund survey in 1995 revealed that whilst churches generally endorsed holistic mission, some uncertainty still prevailed as to the relationship between evangelism and social action.

There was a feeling that many church members still saw mission primarily as preaching the gospel, even though there was conviction about the distinctive nature of Christian relief and development (that is, Christians have something unique to offer which the secular agencies cannot).

Whilst convinced that Christians should act in the face of injustice, less people were convinced about the wisdom of political involvement.[6] This does not have to remain the case. You and your team's efforts to include the needs of the Third-World in your programme of bringing the world to your church *can make a difference*. It is well worth the extra time and effort involved.

Further reading

Dear Life (Christian Aid 1998). A prayer handbook with a difference.

Proclaim Liberty (Christian Aid 1998). Reflections on theology and debt.

Fair trade/ ethical lifestyle

The Good Life (World Development Movement, 1998).

Sir Cliff Richard and Steve Chalke, *Get up and Give* (Harper Collins, 1998).

Tearcraft Catalogue.

Traidcraft Catalogue.

Specific issues

Glenn Myers *Children in Crisis* (OM Publishing, 1998).

Tim Chester and Ian Roberts *The Arms Trade* (Tearfund, Public Affairs Briefing no. 4, April 1996).

Tim Chester *The Chains of Injustice* (Tearfund, 1996/97).

Tim Chester *Landmines. The Hidden Enemy* (Tearfund Public Affairs Briefing no. 2, August 1994).

Tim Chester *Third-World Debt* (Tearfund, Public Affairs Briefing no.1, 3rd ed., Oct. 1995).

The commercial sexual exploitation of street children (World Vision, June 1996).

Campaigns

For details of ongoing campaigns on behalf of the poor and the exploited, which aim to challenge and change government and company policies, contact Christian Aid; World Development Movement; Jubilee 2000; Tearfund.

Footnotes

1. *The commercial sexual exploitation of street children* (World Vision's UK Special Report, June 1996), p.5. Quoted with permission.

2. *The Arms Trade*, (Tearfund), p.3.

3. *Landmines: The hidden enemy*, (Tearfund), p.4.

4. Tim Chester, *The Chains of Injustice*, p.3.

5. A. Roberts and R. Pendrey; *Radipole Relay*, Dec. 1996/Jan. 1977. Reproduced by permission of Mission Romania.

6. *Mission and the poor* (Tearfund, July 1995), p.18.

Epilogue'

Out of breath and overwhelmed?

I wonder if you are thinking, 'Well that's all very well in theory, but what about in practice? Who do you think we are!'

Panic not! You are not expected to attempt everything in this book. Remember, it is a pick'n'mix of ideas, not a compulsory twelve-day assault course.

Not everything in this book will be suitable for your situation, and some things may never be possible to try out. I hope, however, that you will have found some helpful suggestions which will inspire you to dream dreams and attempt great things for God right here at home.

In Galatians 6:9 the apostle Paul exhorts Christians not to grow tired of helping other people, and reassures them they will be rewarded in due course, if they persevere.

Think about it. Helping other people is what being a mission mobiliser is all about: helping your church to understand and respond to the needs of world-mission; helping missionaries by raising interest and support for them; helping the people whom those missionaries serve. The support which you are instrumental in raising is vital in making world-mission possible.

It is easy to start off enthusiastically, but it is the continuing effort which really counts. Being an effective mission mobiliser requires sustained effort, commitment, perseverance in the face of apathy, and lots of imagination. This is not easy to keep up over a long period of time, especially if you are largely on your own and do not have the help and support of a good team or the enthusiastic backing of a leadership who share the vision.

The job you are doing is one of the most important in any Christian group. Whatever your situation humanly speaking, God is on your side. He sees your role as a vital ingredient in your group's corporate life, and necessary for their very existence. Without vision, especially a missionary vision, towards the neighbourhood, nation and world, the people of God slowly and surely perish.

There may be times when you, like me, meet a wall of blank stares and little response.

It can be difficult to keep on enthusing about mission when hardly anyone seems to be listening, especially when you are trying so hard, preparing well and doing all the right things. When all your energy and ideas seem to get nowhere it is tempting to take the easy way out and do the minimum for the sake of a quiet life.

It is not all doom and gloom, however. Far from it! Raising interest in mission can be inspiring, and thrilling. The more you get involved, the more you will want to do.

With more than a billion people in our world today who have not yet heard the Gospel, and a thousand people groups amongst whom there is very little Christian work, there is still much to do.

Be encouraged. Be faithful. In his time, by his Spirit, there will be a harvest.

On behalf of the sending organisations, the missionaries and the people whom they serve in the name of Christ, 'Thank you.' Where would they be without you?

May God inspire and empower you as you engage in bringing the world, his world, to your church.

Directory

Contents

DIRECTORY (Please enclose an SAE with any initial written enquiries to these organisations).

I. AGENCIES DIRECTLY SUPPORTING, RESOURCING AND TRAINING NATIONAL CHRISTIANS

Amen
108, Station Road, Crayford, Kent DA1 3QG

WorldShare
Bawtry Hall, Bawtry, Doncaster DN10 6JH
Tel. 01302 710273 Fax. 01302 710027
E-mail: 100657.147@compuserve.com
Web-site: http://www.worldshare.org.uk

II. INFORMATION, RESOURCES AND TRAINING

Administry
PO Box 57, St Albans AL1 3DT
Tel. 01727 856370 Fax. 01727 843765
E-mail: administry@ibm.net

Chime Worldwide
11A, Upper Teddington Road,
Kingston upon Thames, Surrey KT1 4DL
Tel. 020 8977 5899 Fax. 020 8977 5899

Christian Computer Art
33, Bramley Way, Hardwick, Cambridge CB3 7XD
Tel. 01954 210009

Christian Research
Vision Building, 4, Footscray Road,
Eltham, London SE9 2TZ
Tel. 020 8294 1989 Fax. 020 8294 0014
E-mail: admin@christian-research.org.uk
Web-site: christian-research.org.uk
Web-site: ukchristianhandbook.org.uk

Christian Vocations
Holloway Street West, Lower Gornal, Dudley,
West Midlands DY3 2DZ
Tel. 01902 882836 Fax. 01902 881099
E-mail: info@christianvocations.org
Web-site: http://www.christianvocations.org/

Christians Abroad
Suite 233, Bon Marché Centre,
241-251 Ferndale Road, London
Tel. 020 7346 5956 Fax. 020 7346 5955
E-mail: admin@cabroad.org.uk
Web-site: http://www.cabroad.org.uk

World Service Enquiry
Tel. 02027 346 5950 Fax. 02027 346 5955
E-mail: wse@cabroad.org.uk

Echoes of Service
1, Widcombe Crescent, Bath BA2 6AQ
Tel. 01225 310 893 / 480 635 Fax. 01225 480 134

Global Connections
(formerly Evangelical Missionary Alliance)
Whitefield House, 186, Kennington Park Road,
London SE11 4BT
Tel. 0207 207 2156 Fax. 0207 207 2159
E-mail: info@globalconnections.co.uk
Web-site: http://www.globalconnections.co.uk

International Training Network
Exchange Buildings, Upper Hinton Road,
Bournemouth, Dorset BH1 2HH
Tel/Fax. 01202 789089
E-mail: len-grates@compuserve.com

Mission Computers
Manor Farm, 14 Alms Hill, Bourn, Cambridge CB3 7SH
Tel. 01954 718076 Fax. 01954 719703
E-mail: thebook@miscom.co.uk
Web-site: http://www.miscom.co.uk

Radstock
2a, Argyle Street, Mexborough,
South Yorkshire S64 9BW
Tel. 01709 582345 Fax. 01709 583202
E-mail: 100540.1645@compuserve.com

The Missionary Training Service
Flat 5, 40 Buckingham Gate, London SW1E 6BS
Tel./ Fax. 020 7932 0728
E-mail: coord@missionarytraining.org
Web-site: http://www.missionarytraining.org

St. John's Extension Studies
Chilwell Lane, Bramcote, Nottingham NG9 3DS
Tel. 0115 925 1117 Fax. 0115 943 6438

Sunrise Software
PO Box 19, Carlisle CA3 0HP
Tel. 0845 0579 579 Fax. 01228 514949
E-mail: sales@sunrise-software.com
Web-site: http://www.sunrise-software.com

TASK (Training and Advice for Service in the Kingdom)
13, School Road, Bradenham, Thetford IP25 7QU
Tel. 01760 440 200
E-mail: roger@taskgb.freeserve.co.uk

III. MISSION AGENCIES

AIM International (Africa Inland Mission)
2, Vorley Road, Archway, London N19 5HE
Tel. 020 7281 1184 Fax. 020 7281 4479
E-mail: uk@aim-eur.org
Web-site: http://www.aim-us.org

Assemblies of God: World Ministries Office
IBTI Hook Place, Burgess Hill, West Sussex RH15 8RF
Tel. 01444 48383 Fax. 01444 236038

BMS World Mission
PO Box 49, Baptist House, 129, Broadway,
Didcot, Oxon. OX11 8XA
Tel. 01235 517700 (switchboard),
01235 517617 (mission & publicity resources).
Fax. 01235 517601
E-mail: mail@bms.org.uk (for general emails);
resources@bms.org.uk (mission & publicity resources)
Web-site: http://www.bms.org.uk

CMS (Church Missionary Society)
Partnership House, 157, Waterloo Road,
London SE1 8UU
Tel. 020 7928 8681 Fax. 020 7401 3215
E-mail: info@cms-uk.org
Web-site: http://www.cms-uk.org

Crosslinks
251, Lewisham Way, London SE4 1XF
Tel. 020 8691 6111 Fax. 020 8694 8023
E-mail: janeth@crosslinks.org

Elim International Office
PO Box 38, Cheltenham, Glos. GL50 3HN
Tel. 01242 519904 Fax. 01242 542023
E-mail: missions@elimhq.com
Web-site: http://www.elim.org.uk

FEBA Radio
Ivy Arch Road, Worthing, West Sussex BN14 8BX
Tel. 01903 237281 Fax. 01903 205294
E-mail: reception@febaradio.org.uk
Web-site: http://www.feba.org.uk

Interserve
325, Kennington Road, London SE11 4QH
Tel. 020 7735 8227 Fax. 020 7587 5362
E-mail: isewi@isewi.globalnet.co.uk
Web-site: http://www.interserve.org

Latin Link
175 Tower Bridge Road, London SE1 2AB
Tel. 020 7939 9000 Fax. 020 7939 9015
E-mail: UKoffice@latinlink.org
Web-site: http://www.latinlink.org/latinlink/

The Leprosy Mission
Goldhay Way, Orton Goldhay, Peterborough PE2 5GZ
Tel. 01733 370505 Fax. 01733 370960
E-mail: post@tlmew.org.uk
Web-site: http://www.leprosymission.org/

MAF (Mission Aviation Fellowship)
Ingles Manor, Castle Hill Avenue,
Folkestone, Kent CT20 2TN
Tel. 01303 850950 Fax. 01303 852800
E-mail: maf-uk@maf-uk.org
Web-site: http://www.maf.org

The Methodist World Church Office
25, Marylebone Road, London NW1 5JR
Tel. 020 7486 5502 Fax. 020 7935 1507

OM (Operation Mobilisation)
The Quinta, Weston Rhyn, Oswestry,
Shropshire SY10 7LT
Tel. 01691 773388 Fax. 01691 778378
E-mail: info@uk.om.org
Web-site: http://www.uk.om.org

OMF International (Overseas Missionary Fellowship)
Station Approach, Borough Green,
Sevenoaks, Kent TN15 8BG
Tel. 01732 887 299 Fax. 01732 887 224
E-mail: omf@omf.org.uk
Web-site: http://www.omf.org.uk

SAMS (South American Missionary Society)
Allen Gardiner House, 12, Fox Hill,
Birmingham B29 4AG
Tel. 0121 472 2616 Fax. 0121 472 7977
E-mail: samsgb@compuserve.com
Web-site: http://www.samsgb.org

SIM UK (Society for International Ministries)
Wetheringsett Manor, Wetheringsett,
Stowmarket, Suffolk IP14 5QX
Tel. 01449 766464 Fax. 01449 767148
E-mail: postmast@sim.co.uk
Web-site: http://www.sim.org

USPG
(United Society for the Propagation of the Gospel)
Partnership House, 157, Waterloo Road,
London SE1 8XA
Tel. 020 7928 8681 Fax. 020 7928 2371
E-mail: enquiries@uspg.org.uk

WEC International
Bulstrode, Oxford Road, Gerrards Cross,
Bucks. SL9 8SZ
Tel. 01753 884 631 Fax. 01753 882 470
E-mail: 100546.1550@compuserve.com
Web-site: http://www.cin.co.uk/wec

World Horizons
Centre for the Nations, North Dock, Llanelli SA15 2LF
Tel. 01554 750 005 Fax. 01554 773 304
E-mail: ndoc@whorizons.org
Web-site: http://www.whorizons.org

Wycliffe Bible Translators
Horsleys Green, High Wycombe, Bucks. HP14 3XL
Tel. 01494 482521 Fax. 01494 483297
E-mail: general_uk_delivery@wycliffe.org
Web-site: http://www.wycliffe.org.uk

YWAM (Youth with a Mission)
13, Highfield Oval, Ambrose Lane,
Harpenden, Herts. AL5 4BX
Tel. 01582 463 300 Fax. 01582 463 213
E-mail: enquiries@oval.com
Web-site: http://www.ywam-england.com

IV. RELIEF AND DEVELOPMENT AGENCIES AND
CAMPAIGN CO-ORDINATORS

ARC (Aid to Russion Christians)
PO Box 200, Bromley, Kent BR1 1QF
Tel. 020 8460 6046 Fax. 020 8466 1244
E-mail: arcladybird@compuserve.com

CAFOD (Catholic Fund for Overseas Development)
Romero Close, Stockwell Road, London SW9 9TY
Tel. 020 7733 7900 Fax. 020 7274 9630
E-mail: hq@cafod.org.uk
Web-site: http://www.cafod.org.uk

Christian Aid
PO Box 100, London SE1 7RT
Tel. 020 7620 4444 Fax. 020 7620 0719
E-mail: info@christian-aid.org
Web-site: http://www.christian-aid.org.uk

CORD (Christian Outreach Relief and Development)
1, New Street, Leamington Spa,
Warwickshire CV31 1HP
Tel. 01926 315301 Fax. 01926 885786
E-mail: cord_uk@compuserve.com

European Christian Mission
50, Billing Road, Northampton NN1 5DH
Tel. 01604 621092 Fax. 01604 20594
E-mail: ECMBritain@compuserve.com
Web-site: http://www.ecmi.org

Link Romania (See Partnership for Growth below.)

Love Russia
Falcon House, 3, Castle Road, Newport,
Isle of Wight PO30 1DL
Tel/Fax. 01983 530262
E-mail: love.russia@ukonline.co.uk

Mission Without Borders
Lakeside Pavilion, Chaucer Business Park, Kemsing,
Sevenoaks, Kent TN15 6QY
Tel. 01732 765200 Fax. 01732 765208

Oasis Trust
115, Southwark Bridge Road, London SE1 0AX
Tel. 020 7450 9000 Fax. 020 7450 9001
E-mail: OasisTrust@compuserve.com

One World Week
P.O. Box 2555, Reading, Berkshire RG1 4XW
Tel. 0118 939 4933
E-mail: enquiries@oneworldweek.org
Web-site: http://www.oneworldweek.org

Operation Christmas Child
PO Box 732, Wrexham, Clwyd LL13 9ZA
Tel. 01978 660465 Fax. 01978 660294

Partnership for Growth
Link House, 59/61 Lyndhurst Road, Worthing,
West Sussex BN11 2DB
Tel. 01903 529333 Fax. 01903 529007
E-mail: linkrom@linkrom.org
Web-site: http://www.linkrom.org

Samaritan's Purse International
Victoria House, Victoria Road,
Buckhurst Hill, Essex IG9 5EX
Tel. 020 8559 2044 Fax. 020 2502 9062
E-mail: 100067.1226@compuserve.com
Web-site: http://www.samaritans-purse.org.uk

Tearfund
100, Church Road, Teddington, Middlesex TW11 8QE
Tel. 020 8977 9144 Fax. 020 8943 3594
(0845 355 8355 for general enquiries)
E-mail: enquiry@tearfund.dircon.co.uk
Web-site: http://www.tearfund.org.

Traidcraft plc
Kingsway, Gateshead, Tyne and Wear NE11 0NE
Tel. 0191 491 0591 Fax. 0191 482 2690

WDM (World Development Movement)
25, Beehive Place, London SW9 7BR
Tel. 020 7737 6215 Fax. 020 7274 8232
E-mail: wdm@wdm.org.uk
Web-site: http://www.wdm.org.uk

World Vision
599 Avebury Boulevard, Milton Keynes MK9 3PG
Tel. 01908 841007 Fax. 01908 841001
E-mail: info@worldvision.org.uk
Web-site: http://www.worldvision.org.uk

V. OVERSEAS STUDENTS/ ETHNIC MINORITIES

IFES (International Fellowship of Evangelical Students)
Kennett House,108 London Road,
Headington, Oxford OX3 9AW
Tel. 01865 308801 Fax. 01865 308802
email: ifes@ibm.net

ISCS (International Student Christian Services)
3, Crescent Stables, 139 Upper Richmond Road,
London SW15 2TN
Tel. 020 8780 3511 Fax. 020 8785 1174
E-mail: info@iscs.org.uk
Web-site: http://www.iscs.org.uk

London City Mission
(organise Tell a Tourist in summer)
175, Tower Bridge Road, London. SE1 2AH
Tel. 020 7407 7585 Fax. 020 7403 6711
E-mail: lcm.uk@btinternet.com

Word of Life
Post Box 14, Oldham. OL1 3WW

VI. SUPPORT AGENCIES

Adopt-a-Child
PO Box 5589 Inverness IV2 7WG
Tel. 01463 792600
Fax. 01463 711926 'by request'
E-mail: info@adopt-a-child.org.uk
Web-site: http://www.adopt-a-child.org.uk

Bientot (Branch of WEC. Distribute Gospel paper in
French to French speaking countries worldwide.)
Unit 6, Garcia Trading Estate, Canterbury Road,
Worthing, West Sussex BN13 1AL
Tel. 01903 690112

Book Aid (Send new and second-hand
Christian books overseas.)
Head Office: 271, Church Road, London SE19 2QQ
Warehouse/bookshop: Mayeswood Road,
Grove Park, London SE12
Tel. 020 8857 7794

Other **Book Aid** shops: Bawtry Hall, Ranskill,
Barnard Castle, and Templepatrick (N. Ireland).

British and Overseas Optical Missions
(Send used spectacles abroad.)
8, Kenilworth Avenue, Wimbledon,
London SW19 7LN
Tel. 020 8946 5281

Child Rescue International (See Mission Without
Borders International in section IV.)

Missionary Mart
99, Woodmansterne Road, Carlshalton,
Surrey SM5 4EG
Tel. 020 8643 3616 / Warehouse 020 8669 3495

Northwood Missionary Auctions
Freepost, Northwood, Middlesex HA6 1BR
Tel. 01978 836 634

SOON (Branch of WEC. Distribute evangelistic broad-
sheets and Bible courses in easy English worldwide.)
44, Twyford Road, Willington, Derby DE65 6BN
Tel. 01283 702334 Fax. 01283 702334
E-mail: admin@soon.org.uk
Web-site (online magazine): http://www.soon.org.uk

Stamps for Evangelism
11, St. John's Drive, Chaddesden, Derby DE21 6SD
Tel/ Fax. 01332 663 270

TWAM (Tools With a Mission)
Unit 3, Perry Barn, Burstall Lane,
Sproughton, Ipswich IP8 3DJ
Tel. 01473 652 029 Fax. 01473 652 029

UPESI (A branch of WEC. Distribute broadsheet
in Swahili to Africa.)
44, Twyford Road, Willington, Derby DE65 6BN
Tel. 01283 702334 Fax. 01283 702334

Wallington Missionary Auctions
20, Dalmeny Road, Carlshalton, Surrey SM5 4PP
Tel. 020 8647 8437

Workaid (Send refurbished tools and sewing
machines overseas.)
Unit 2b, St.Georges Industrial Estate, White Lion
Road, Amersham, Bucks. HP7 9JQ
Tel. 01494 765506 Fax. 01494 765507
E-mail: workaid@btclick.com
Web-site: http://www.home.btclick.com/workaid

Wycliffe Associates (Opportunities for Christians to
use their skills to support missionaries and world-
mission from home.)
7, Conwy Street, Rhyl, Denbighshire LL18 3ET
Tel. 01745 343 300 E-mail: wa-uk@iname.com

VII. Web-sites with listings/ links.

Christian Missions Homepage: http://www.sim.org

SOON missions page:
http://www.webauthors.org/guide/webmission.html

Please note that the organisations and resource
materials mentioned in this book represent just a
fraction of those in existence. Inclusion or ommision is
not intended to reflect any value judgement of any
organisation's orthodoxy or merit on my part.

Bibliography

Barnett, Betty, *Friend Raising: Building a missionary support team that lasts* (YWAM publishing, 1991).

Benson, Ian E. (ed.), *The Effective Sending Church.* Booklet 7. The Missionary Training Series (The Missionary Training Service, 1997).

Bowen, Roger, . . . *so I Send You: A study guide to mission* (SPCK, 1996).

Brierley, Peter and Wraight, Heather, (eds.), *The UK Christian Handbook Millennium Edition* (Christian Research/ Harper Collins Religious, 1999).

Burgess, Lynne, *Creative Display* (Scholastic Publications, 1991).

Butler, Tom and Butler, Barbara, *Just Mission* (Mowbray, 1993).

Casson, Herbert N.C, *Window Display* (Tynron Press, 1990).

Collins, Marjorie A., *Manual for Today's Missionary: From recruitment to retirement* (William Carey Library, USA,1986).

Cooper, Anne, *Heart to Heart: Talking with Moslem friends* (Word of Life, 1997).

Cooper, Anne, *Ismael my Brother* (Marc, 1993).

Cundy, Mary, *Better than the Witchdoctor* (Monarch,1994).

Dillon, William P., *People Raising. A practical guide to raising support* (Moody Press, USA, 1993).

Dimensions of the Voluntary Sector (Charities Aid Foundation, 1998).

Foyle, Marjory F., *Honourably Wounded: Stress amongst Christian workers* (Marc, 1987).

Garrett, Willis E., *You can have a Successful Missionary Program in your Church* (SIM, Canada, 1991).

Gately, Ian and Gately, Jean, *My Reasonable Service?* (Pentland Press, 1995).

Gaukroger, Stephen, *Why Bother with Mission?* (IVP, 1996).

Goldsmith, Elizabeth, *Getting from there to here* (OM Publishing, rev. edn. 1995).

— — — — — — -*Roots and Wings: Five generations and their influence* (OM Publishing, 1998).

Goldsmith, Martin, *Life's Tapestry: Reflections and insights from my life* (OM Publishing, 1997).

Goldsmith, Martin (ed.), *Love your Local Missionary* (Marc, 1984).

Griffiths, Michael, *A Task Unfinished* (Monarch, 1996).

— — — — — — -*Cinderella with Amnesia* (IVP, 1975).

———————- *Get your Church Involved in Missions* (OMF Books, 1972).

———————- *What on Earth are you Doing?* (IVP, 1983).

Griffiths, Michael (ed.), *Ten Sending Churches* (Marc, 1985).

International Directory of Voluntary Work (Vacation Work Publications, 1997).

Johnstone, Jill, *You can Change the World* (WEC, 1992).

Johnstone, Patrick, *Operation World* (WEC, 1993).

———————- *The Church is Bigger than you Think* (Christian Focus Publications / WEC, 1998).

Jordan, Peter, *Re-entry: Making the transition from missions to life at home* (YWAM Publishing, 1992).

Kane, J. Herbert, *Winds of Change in the Christian Mission* (Moody Press, USA, 1973).

Kenney, Betty Jo, *The Missionary Family* (William Carey Library, USA, 1983).

Lyon, David H. S., *How Foreign is Mission?* (The Saint Andrew Press, 1978).

Morgan, Helen, *Who'd be a Missionary?* (Patmos, 1965).

———————- *Who'd Stay a Missionary?* (Patmos, 1971).

Musk, Bill, *The Unseen Face of Islam: Sharing the Gospel with ordinary Muslims* (Marc, 1989).

Myers, Glenn, *Children in Crisis* (Briefings, OM Publishing, 1998).

———————- *The Arab World* (Briefings, OM Publishing, 1998).

———————- *The World Christian Starter Kit* (WEC, 1993).

Northcott, Michael, *Life after Debt: Christianity and Global Justice* (SPCK, 1999).

O'Donnell, Kelly (ed.), *Missionary Care: Counting the cost for world evangelization* (William Carey Library, USA, 1992).

Peacock, David and Weaver, Geoff (eds.), *World Praise: Songs from around the world* (Marshall Pickering, 1993).

Perspectives on the World Christian Movement (1981, William Carey Library, USA: rev.edn.1992).

Pirolo, Neal, *Serving as Senders: Six ways to support your missionaries.* (OM Publishing, 1997).

Plueddemann, Jim and Plueddemann, Carol, *Witnesses to all the World. God's heart for the nations, 9 studies* (Harold Shaw, USA, 1996).

Prayers Encircling the World (SPCK, 1998).

Prior, Ian (ed.), *The Christian at work Overseas: A manual for those embarking in service overseas,* (Tearfund, 1978).

Ranck, J. Allan, *Education for Mission* (Fellowship Press, USA, 1961).

Rand, Stephen, *Guinea Pig for Lunch* (Hodder & Stoughton, 1998).

Richard, Sir Cliff and Steve Chalke, *Get up and Give* (Harper Collins, 1998).

Sider, Ronald, *Bread of Life - stories of radical mission* (Triangle: SPCK, 1994).

Missions Ideas Notebook. Promoting missions in the local church (SIM, 1975).

Sjogren, Bob, and Stearns, Bill & Amy, *Run with the Vision* (Bethany House Publishers, USA, 1995).

Spraggett, Daphne *You too can Change the World* (WEC, 1996).

Stearns, Bill and Stearns, Amy, *Catch the Vision 2000* (Bethany House Publishers, USA, 1991).

Stepping Out: *A guide to short-term missions* (SMS Publications, USA, 1987).

Sutcliffe, Sally, *Aisha my Sister* (Solway, 1997).

Taylor, Rhena, Rough Edges: *Christians abroad in today's world* (IVP, 1978).

— — — — — —- *The Prisoner and Other Stories: Sharp-edged stories of Africa* (March, 1987).

Tirabissi, Maren C. and Eddy, Kathy Qonson, *Gifts of Many Cultures* (Cleveland, Ohio: United Church Press, 1995).

Thomas, Norman, (ed.), *Readings in World Mission* (SPCK, 1995).

Townsend, Anne, *Faith Without Pretending,* (Hodder and Stoughton, 1990).

Verkuyl, J, *Contemporary Missiology, an introduction,* (Eerdmans, USA, 1978).

Volunteer Work (Central Bureau for Educational Visits and Exchanges, 1995).

Voluntary Agencies Directory (NVCO Publications, 1999).

Wallis, John (ed.), *We Believe in Mission* (Marshalls/ STL, 1983).

Wardell, Margaret and Gidoomal, Ram *Chapatis for Tea: Reaching your Hindu Neighbour: A practical guide* (Highland, 1994).

Whiteford, Rhona, and Fitzsimmons, Jim, *Bright Ideas: Display* (Scholastic Publications, 1988).

Williams, Derek (ed.), *Prepared to Serve* (Tearfund / SU, 1989).

Williamson, Mabel, *Have we no Rights? A frank discussion of Christians' rights* (China Inland Mission, 1958).

Wilson, J.Christy, *Today's Tentmakers: Self support: An alternative model for worldwide witness* (Tyndale House Publishers, USA, 1979).

Woodberry, J. Dudley; Engen, Charles Van and Elliston, Edgar J., *Missiological Education for the 21st Century* (Orbis, 1996).